Outsourcing

... in brief

D1299939

Outsourcing

... in brief

Mike Johnson

Butterworth-Heinemann
Linacre House, Jordan Hill, Oxford OX2 8DP
A division of Reed Educational and Professional Publishing Ltd

℞ A member of the Reed Elsevier plc group

OXFORD   BOSTON   JOHANNESBURG
MELBOURNE   NEW DELHI   SINGAPORE

First published 1997

British Library Cataloguing in Publication Data
A catalogue record for this book is available from the British Library

Library of Congress Cataloguing in Publication Data
A catalogue record for this book is available from the British Library

ISBN 0 7506 2876 6

Typeset by Avocet Typeset, Brill, Aylesbury, Bucks
Printed and bound in Great Britain by
Biddles Ltd, Guildford and King's Lynn

Contents

Preface

Outsourcing isn't new. What's new is the recent emphasis that has been put on sub-contracting non-core business, particularly in two areas – information technology (IT) and facilities management (FM). This book is intended as a non-technical review of where outsourcing stands today and provides an overview of what we can all learn from the organizations, consultants and academics who have practised or studied it.

From the considerable desk research and face-to-face interviews that make up this book, it is clear that outsourcing is not just another passing management fad – if it is applied correctly – but a powerful management process that can reap huge benefits for those with the courage and the professionalism to get their organizational equations right. Often outsourcing is seen in the same critical light as downsizing – a quick-fix, cost-cutting tool. But in the hands of the right management it can be a true strategic weapon, that can pervade every corner of the management process – bringing prosperity and secure futures to many.

I hope that this book will provide practical insights into what outsourcing can achieve and will act as a useful guide as to how to make a start in developing, assessing and practising an outsourcing policy. And one other thing! I hope it will serve to define what outsourcing – or sourcing as many now want to call it – really is; as there is some serious confusion among many top managers – many of whom it appears have never even heard of the term.

In the midst of our research into this book we were amused to see a reference to a survey by the market research firm MORI of UK chief executives, that showed many not only didn't know what outsourcing was, but didn't know that their organizations had been practising it for years! Part of the reason for our amusement was we had just completed an interview with a very senior banker in London on his bank's outsourcing programme – having been sent to do so by their public relations company – who refused to let us use them as a case study on the grounds that what they were doing 'wasn't outsourcing' when clearly it was!

To everyone who reads this book, I hope it gives you a much clearer understanding of what outsourcing is and what it can and cannot do for your business. It is a growing phenomenon that no one can afford to ignore and may you have much success with it.

Mike Johnson
Largs, Ayrshire, Scotland 1997

A special note of appreciation

The content of this book owes a great deal to the enthusiasm and encouragement of the Outsourcing Institute in New York, and particularly their co-founder, Michael Corbett. Mr Corbett is also President of Michael F. Corbett & Associates Strategic Management Consultancy. His suggestions and guidance – as well as his permission to quote from their research and case material – has helped enormously in the task of providing a complete round-up of the state-of-the-art of outsourcing today.

Acknowledgements

It takes a lot of people to make a book like this work; without the professional input and support of outsourcing practitioners in industry, consulting firms and academia it wouldn't have been possible. However, I would like to particularly acknowledge the very considerable help of Michael F. Corbett, co-founder of the Outsourcing Institute in New York (to whom I referred to further in my Preface) and to Terry Smith of Chi-Chi's International in Brussels and Bob Milne of Hooker Cockram in Australia, who gave up time from very busy global schedules to help the project develop. Additionally Mike Summerfield of Xerox, Harold Lewis of Xephon, Freddy Nurski of ISS, Helen Blake of Andersen Consulting, Sarah Blake of PA Consulting, Leslie Willcocks of Templeton College Oxford, Fari Akhlaghi of Sheffield Hallam University, Stephanie Gray of HMSO for permission to use material from the KPMG/Impact study, Gail Hartley of Mowlem Facilities Management, Kevan Wooden of Procordia, Karen Fletcher of Sanders & Sidney, Colin Bannerman of Texaco, and Sandra Lester of The Conference Board in Brussels were all of considerable assistance.

Finally, I would like to make a special point of thanking my researcher for this project, Bodil Jones. Without her hard work, enthusiasm, late nights and persuasive arguments on countless phone calls, faxes, letters and e-mails this book would never have been written. In my own small way, outsourcing much of the research for this book shows that – if managed correctly as a partnership – the concept works very well indeed.

Mike Johnson is a consultant and author based in Brussels, Belgium. He founded Johnson & Associates SA, in 1982, specializing in international corporate affairs, corporate editorial projects and research programmes for multinational corporations and institutions around the world. A regular monthly columnist for the international magazine *Management Consulting*, where he writes on global management trends, he is also the International Editor of the US monthly *Management Review* and Managing Editor of *Global Management* and *Global Management Asia Pacific*. In addition, he is the author of the best-selling books *Managing in the Next Millennium* (published in 1995 and translated into seven languages), *Getting a GRIP on Tomorrow* and *The Aspiring Manager's Guide to Survival* (both published in 1996). A further book, *Teleworking*, is published as part of this 'in brief' series.

Working with his team of writers and researchers in Brussels, Mike Johnson has carried out consulting and editorial assignments across Europe, the Middle East, North America and Asia. He is a frequent speaker at business functions, conferences and seminars and a successful workshop leader on corporate communication issues. He has worked extensively with both large multinationals (IBM, ITT, Mobil, DHL, General Electric) as well as many international consulting groups and institutions.

1

In search of the source

Commentators such as Jon Averbach and Russell Baker, among others (see quotes) have managed to give the act of outsourcing a very mixed reputation indeed. Seen by those outside business – and many toiling on the lower slopes of the industrial pyramid – as yet another arcane device thought up by heads of corporations to yield ever greater profits at the expense of workers and middle managers, outsourcing as a concept is badly in need of some public relations. In the majority of reports – even those by business and management publications – outsourcing has been given a big black reject stamp and lumped together with downsizing and business process reengineering (BPR) as a bad news, bad vibe fad, that – while it may eventually go away – is going to cause a great deal of death and destruction before it does.

But while it may be looked at askance by many, outsourcing is too important a concept to be dismissed out of hand as another way to enrich shareholders at the expense of workers. While it may well be true that the majority of corporations base their first decision to outsource on the need to cut costs, it is a growing phenomenon that – like other trends – can work very well indeed if it is applied properly. The trouble is the reports about outsourcing are of the organizations that didn't do it all that well. The world, it would seem, loves to dwell on mistakes, miscalculations and misery rather than sympathy and success. For, just as many business professionals – especially those hard pressed to squeeze more profit and productivity out of their companies – misread the concept of BPR (by failing to read the instructions in the second part of all the books written about it!) and conse-

Outsourcing

quently only got to the downsizing part, outsourcing is not a quick fix. Indeed the worst time to do it, many observers say, is when most companies start – when the profits start to plunge. And in the process of using outsourcing to halt or reverse a profit slide, outsourcing gets – deservedly – a bad, bad name. Referred to by Alan Cane in an article in the *Financial Times* as 'painted by some as the data processing equivalent of selling the family silver', it is often worse than that. Something like instead of the fox getting into the hen house, letting him (or her) take the hen house home.

in brief

'... outsourcing is something almost all big computer manufacturers do, but few admit. It's like buying a frozen pie for a dinner party to avoid the hassle of rolling out the dough; few chefs care to divulge that it's not home-made.' – **Jon Auerbach**, *The Boston Globe*

Part of the image problem of outsourcing is that it is a made-up word that joins the long list of fads and furbelows that have cluttered the business and management firmament like showers of meteors over the past forty years. People – and that means anyone without the title of director or vice president – no longer trust new words – especially when you can possibly link them to the distribution of little pink slips as redundancy notices tend to be called.

And that is just the issue. One side sees downsizing, BPR and outsourcing activity as a natural part of doing business in today's complex, global village. The other side see outsourcing as just another frightening word they have to learn, but they know instinctively won't do them any good. As *New*

In search of the source

York Times columnist Russell Baker says, 'If you sat for 40 days and 40 nights in a lonely room trying to guess what outsourcing might be, what are the chances you would see a great tycoon firing the local workforce to take advantage of cheap labour in other towns and countries?'

Baker's often acerbic words tell a sort of truth, but that is seen from the USA. In a Europe still being pummelled by job losses – with little end in sight – workforces on hearing the word 'outsourcing' might not instinctively know what it means, but I am sure they would think it wasn't going to be a good thing for them.

in brief '... the existence of a secret euphemism factory to which captains of industry resort when they require new ways of downplaying the negative with silly words like "outsourcing".' – **Russell Baker, *The International Herald Tribune***

What all this means is that in examining outsourcing as a phenomenon that is already affecting the lives of virtually all of us in the so-called Western world, it is important to separate what it really is – what outsourcing really does – into two distinct parts. Part one is a social and economic understanding, because whatever outsourcing's supporters may say, it does bring with it disruption and rapid change to long-practised ways of work. Part two is what outsourcing means to organizations, how they implement it and what results they can expect from the process. Without an appreciation of both parts of the outsourcing equation managers who jump in too quickly are in danger of making major mistakes – especially in lowering the morale of an already mistrustful and jittery workforce – that, like marrying in haste, they can only repent at their leisure. Likewise, other employees and industry observers will never give outsourcing the hearing that in this rapidly moving world it deserves.

Luckily, it isn't all doom and gloom out there in the real

Outsourcing

world. First, outsourcing as a concept is changing – *fast*! Second, there are many responsible companies that are implementing outsourcing processes where they can not only make a difference but take most of their people along for the ride as well. Sure, some might fall off the corporate roller-coaster along the way, but the owners have made certain there's a safety net to break their fall, so they won't come to too much harm.

And in this lies the secret – there is a responsible, moral way to outsource that is being practised by many for the overall good of the company and all its stakeholders. Certainly it doesn't get achieved without some upheaval, but it does offer an alternative to being uncompetitive or going into terminal decline, while still giving as many as possible of the workforce a sound future.

Around the world, companies of all shapes and sizes and all types of industries are coming to terms with new ways of doing business of which outsourcing is an ever-increasing part. But the key reason that outsourcing is changing is that it isn't based simply on lower price, it is based on perceived quality and the type of fit an organization can make: does its culture integrate with your own or just grate?

Just what is outsourcing?

But if outsourcing is ever going to get anywhere – ever going to spruce up its slightly seedy image – the first thing it needs to do is make itself understood as a business term. Right now, today, few people can tell you what outsourcing really is and what it covers. In fact there are so many alternative names for it – from rival factions in many cases – that it is in danger of vanishing as a term in a dust cloud of confusion. Modernists – and, I suspect, a phalanx of consulting firms – have in fact already moved ahead and redefined outsourc-ing. In a historical first, they have actually managed to shorten the term (where normally they add three more words to qualify it as a true trend!) to the simple word *sourcing*. The modernist management gurus claim that under this umbrella is everything you do. You can source outside, but you can source inside as well. Indeed a manager's job is to find the most practical, productive, cost-effective source to getting a job done, a product made, an idea developed. Sadly, a long way behind come other words and phrases which are linked

In search of the source

to outsourcing at one time or another and all are still current in certain countries and industries.

Michael Corbett, formerly the Director of Research and Member Programs at the US-based Outsourcing Institute, who provided a wealth of insight and input into this project, says that 'there are a great number of terms that all boil down to outsourcing in one way or another. The problem is that they often carry other meanings as well!' Corbett's list is not exhaustive but he gets to eleven other words and phrases within seconds: 'sub-contracting, contracting-out, staff augmentation, flexible staffing, employee leasing, professional services, contract programming, facilities maintenance or management, contract manufacturing and contract services.'

A study by the international technical and market research organization Xephon, who specialize exclusively in information systems for large enterprises, noted that 'so many definitions have been used for the terms "outsourcing" and "facilities management" that some care is needed not to make wrong assumptions about what they mean in articles and reports. Indeed, a recent special report in the *Financial Times* on these topics contained many pages that were not in any way related to computing, but to services like catering and building maintenance.'

It helps to make sure that whoever you are dealing with in the outsourcing business understands clearly your definitions otherwise major confusion can arise. It may sound simple – *it's not*!

Defining outsourcing – a tough prospect

One of the problems of outsourcing's image is that no-one seems quite sure what it really is and the extent of activities it covers. In a recent study, *Outsourcing HR Services*, the international business organization, The Conference Board, gave their version – at least as far as human resource activity was concerned. 'To many employers, service outsourcing implies a transfer of an administrative responsibility to an outside organization, an arrangement that changes both service delivery and internal staffing patterns. Contracts with consulting firms, however, are also viewed by some as a form of outsourcing, particularly when close ties

Outsourcing

develop in long-term relationships. Anne Melanson, executive vice-president of human resources and operations at Backer Spielvogel Bates, considers it outsourcing if the work performed by a consultant would otherwise require additional staff. 'Alternatively, an independent contractor, such as a former employee, may be engaged to perform a specific service, which the company may describe as outsourcing. But, as an individual, the contractor can often resemble an employee more than an outsider because the company is able to exercise considerable control over that relationship. Temporary employees, especially those hired through an outside agency, are yet another form of outsourcing. The concept of outsourcing is further complicated when only pieces of a function, rather than an entire service, are contracted out. Training and development is a good example. Many firms use outside teachers or join forces with local educational institutions to deliver some courses for their employees. But many also retain in-house, or very closely control, programmes that focus on company-specific issues or leadership development.'

Being in the information technology (IT) market, which is never sure if it should be the information systems (IS) market, Xephon has cause for concern. However, they need to realize that outsourcing and particularly the often-used term 'facilities management' are part of a much bigger picture than the computer industry. But Xephon's own definitions of the different aspects of the outsourcing process – albeit based on the IT/IS industry – are a useful guide for all of us sailing in these new, uncharted waters. By the way, it helps to make sure that whoever you are dealing with in the outsourcing business understands clearly your definitions, otherwise major confusion can arise. Here's Xephon's definition of outsourcing and related activities:

■ *Outsourcing*: By this we mean contracting out of any service by the IT department [read whatever department you like here], which could range from having all of your development, maintenance and operations performed for you (on a system that could be on your premises or the vendor's) to simply contracting an outside supplier to perform one single, simple task such as to write a program or install a piece of software.

In search of the source

- *Facilities Management (FM)*: In our definition, FM is just one subset of the outsourcing market, where an outside vendor runs your computer operation [read whatever business area you like] for you, either on your premises or theirs. It covers all of the operational and systems programming tasks associated with running a computer system, but not the development and maintenance of applications.

Other common subsets of outsourcing are:

- Applications management, where an outside supplier takes responsibility for the management and maintenance of one, a few, or all of your existing applications.
- Systems integration, where an outsider supplier (or group of suppliers) develops and implements a specific application (or applications) for you, either on new or partially new equipment or on your existing system.
- Simple contracting of outside personnel to help, write, design or test one or more programmes.
- Contracting out systems programming activities to a third party.

Never sign an outsourcing agreement without considering carefully the longer-term implications – too many have, to their regret.

As Xephon themselves say, 'the list is endless' and that is why you need to develop some common understanding of what each term means before you get to doing business with an outsourcing partner, whether you are the giver or the taker of work.

The Outsourcing Institute's Michael Corbett also adds 'consulting' to his list of other terms for outsourcing, but adds, 'although this gets a little fuzzy, because it's such a big bucket'. Big bucket indeed. Outsourcing – and the sons and daughters of outsourcing – are everywhere, covering all types of business and all types of functions. Although IT is seen as one of the main areas of outsourcing, with total office maintenance (known as facilities management – FM) as a close second it doesn't stop there, not by any means. Equally, outsourcing activity is being split into two: manufacturing operations and service providers. Such is the vast differences in what outsourcing can accomplish across the organizational structure that it is beginning to take on very distinct shapes and shades depending what business you are in and how you want to capitalize on the outsourcing trend. This isn't just a phenomenon, it's a many-tentacled

Outsourcing

octopus reaching into every nook and cranny of our businesses. And if it isn't going to go away – at least while the pendulum is still on the upswing – it is a good idea to get to know it and use it – wisely – if we can.

Everyone's an outsourcer

Outsourcing isn't new, it's just the emphasis on it that's changed how we think about it.

One thing we all need to get clear in our heads before we go any further – outsourcing isn't a new idea. The only thing that is new is that the imperatives have changed somewhat and are changing again right now. As individuals we outsource the things we cannot do ourselves or are too busy to do. Just like companies, we rely on our core competencies to survive – hiving off to others with better developed skills in certain areas what we are incapable or unwilling to tackle. Given the time – and possibly the patience – most of us could service our own cars, fix the washing machine and decorate the house. But most of us choose not to because by the time we got around to it our capacity to earn from the things we are good at would be severely reduced and we'd starve to death. And while we may have been able to take our Ford or Volkswagen and change the oil and the spark plugs and the air filter until a decade or so ago, today's engines are so complex that we'd not only need a fully equipped service area but an advanced certificate in automobile mechanics to make any sense of it.

Business life today is just too complicated to do everything in-house. Everyone outsources something – think about it!

Today, in the complex international business world, companies are no different. They too used to be able to fix the things that went broke. They had the time, they had the skills in-house. Today, few organizations – like all of us individuals – have the luxury of time, or much of the latest knowledge. Buying the best on the outside makes sense, as long as it leaves you to concentrate on the things you do best. But if you're in love with fixing the car and you don't do the job you're best at, whether you are an individual or an industry giant – you'll die.

How outsourcing is changing

The New York-based Outsourcing Institute – the leading organization for the study of outsourcing – has shown that in the changing world of today – getting into the process can be split into *tactical* and *strategic* reasons. Comments their executive director, Frank Casale, 'In our ongoing surveys with our 1200 plus member firms, we see the following reasons clearly defined.'

Top five tactical reasons for outsourcing

■ Reduce or control operating costs: By far the single most important reason for outsourcing is to reduce or control operating costs. Access to the outside provider's lower cost structure is one of the most compelling short-term benefits. In a recent Outsourcing Institute survey, companies reported that on average they saw a nine percent reduction in costs through outsourcing.

■ Make capital funds available: Outsourcing reduces the need to invest capital funds in non-core business functions. This makes capital funds more available for core areas. Outsourcing can also improve certain financial measurements of the firm by eliminating the need to show return on equity from capital investments in non-core areas.

■ Cash infusion: Outsourcing can involve the transfer of assets from the customer to the provider. Equipment, facilities, vehicles and licences used in the current operations all have a value and are, in effect, sold to the provider as part of the transaction, resulting in a cash payment.

■ Resources not available internally: Companies outsource because they do not have access to the required resources within. For example, if an organization is expanding its operations, especially into a new geographic area, outsourcing is a viable and important alternative to building the needed capability from the ground up.

Outsourcing

■ Function difficult to manage or out of control: Outsourcing is certainly one option for addressing these types of problems. Outsourcing does not, however, mean abdication of management responsibility, nor does it work well as a knee-jerk reaction by companies in trouble.

Strongly counselling corporations against outsourcing in a panic to shed costs and often people is the Outsourcing Institute's job. But what they have observed is that outsourcing – in the US at least – has now turned a corner, possibly in line with the overall change in the economy. Now, Casale reports, outsourcing is being seen increasingly as a strategic goal and a very important part of the overall direction of the successful organization.

From interviews with member organizations the Outsourcing Institute has listed the following:

Top five strategic reasons for outsourcing
■ Improve business focus: Outsourcing lets the company focus on broader issues while having operational details assumed by an outside expert. For many companies the single most compelling reason for outsourcing is that several of the 'how' type of issues are siphoning off huge amounts of management's resources and attention.
■ Access to world-class capabilities: By the very nature of their specialization, outsourcing providers bring extensive, world-wide, world-class resources to meeting the needs of their customers. According to Norris Overton, vice-president re-engineering at Amtrak, partnering with an organization with world-class capabilities can offer: access to new technology, tools and techniques that the organization may not currently possess; better career opportunities for personnel who transfer to the outsourcing provider; more structured methodologies, procedures and documentation; competitive advantage through expanded skills.
■ Accelerated re-engineering benefits: Outsourcing is often a by-product of another powerful management tool – business process re-engineering

In search of the source

(BPR). It allows an organization to realize immediately the anticipated benefits of re-enegineering by having an outside organization – one that is already re-engineered to world-class standards – take over the process.

■ Shared risks: There are tremendous risks associated with the investments an organization makes. When companies outsource they become more flexible, more dynamic and better able to adapt to changing opportunities.

■ Free resources for other purposes: Every organization has limits on the resources available. Outsourcing permits an organization to redirect its resources from non-core activities towards activities which have the greater return in serving the customer.

These strategic reasons for outsourcing are a key part of the process as well as the passion for change in our organizations. They bear close examination and much, much more than a passing thought.

So what business is saying to itself is 'I know I could do these things if I had to, if I had the time to. But right now, I'm up against the wall and it doesn't make sense to do it myself when I can get it done better, faster and possibly cheaper elsewhere.'

Although squeezing down on costs is consistently cited in industry survey after industry survey as the main reason, the stepping-off point of the outsourcing journey, those that have made the voyage are returning with thrilling tales of lands of new opportunities. It is these tales more than anything else that are driving more and more companies to take up the outsourcing banner.

Outsourcing is being seen less and less as a tactical, cost-saving drive and more and more as a strategic direction that the organization follows.

Corbett's use of the word 'strategic' is significant. Because that is where the main change in outsourcing's focus by the smart money set is leading – from tactical outsourcing to strategic outsourcing.

In ongoing surveys with its 1200 plus membership, the Outsourcing Institute has recorded a major sea change in the way leading companies are viewing outsourcing. Although many chief executives and their staffs still see outsourcing as a means of slashing costs, freeing capital, accessing funds and making up for poor internal resource planning, many corporations are taking outsourcing as a big piece of the

Outsourcing

strategic jig-saw puzzle. Using it to improve business focus, access new capabilities, accelerate organizational change and free valuable resources to pursue new ideas instead of fighting old fires, they are rekindling the excitement within their operations as never before. That's why outsourcing is so important. It is a key part of the whole process of change that all our businesses and institutions are going through – or will ultimately go through in one form or another.

True, in their rush to change, some companies have possibly outsourced too far, too quickly. They are learning their lessons. But if outsourcing is managed well, and the reasons for getting into the process are right, then it can benefit not just the bottom-line but all the stakeholders.

- Instead of facing redundancy, employees can be transferred to more useful work, or retrained with the new outsourced supplier.
- Existing suppliers can increase their overall business involvement.
- Shareholders can expect greater windfalls in dividends.
- Long-term employment and a real future can be made a lot more secure by concentrating on the things the business does well.
- New markets and new opportunities for the people in the business can be opened up by looking for opportunity instead of solving problems.

What most of us have still to take on board in our organizations is that outsourcing, or sourcing, or whatever we want to call it, isn't really – deep down underneath – a faddish trend, it is a way of doing business to meet today's and tomorrow's challenges. While it might be a little excessive to suggest that failure to do it will meet with ultimate corporate tragedy, it is safe to say that if we don't pick it up and examine it from all sides before adopting or rejecting it as a concept we are asking for serious trouble down the line. Most of the reason for that serious trouble will come from the fact that if you or your organization haven't examined outsourcing as an option for parts of your business you may find yourself like the last kid on the block without a bicycle – running to catch up is not a sensible option.

Our friends at the Outsourcing Institute, in their continuing research, have borrowed from others to prepare a set of

In search of the source

selected industry studies that show the extent of outsourcing. Admittedly most of the data is for the USA, but as most US business and management trends eventually travel from east to west, and this phenomenon is no exception, you can expect these numbers to be fairly typical of where Europe – and even Asia – will be in a few years. Also note that a few years have gone past since some of this information was collected.

In business services a 1994 study by Pitney Bowes Management Services of 100 *Fortune 500* corporations found:

- 77 per cent of the firms studied had efforts underway to outsource some aspect of their business.
- 39 per cent of the firms outsourced some or all of their electronic imaging and another 12 per cent expected to do so within two years.
- 7 per cent of the firms outsourced records management with another 14 per cent planning to do so in the next two years.

In logistics a 1994 study by KPMG-Peat Marwick of 309 *Fortune 1000* corporations found:

- 66 per cent outsourced import/export services.
- 63 per cent employed freight brokers for transport selection, carrier monitoring, insurance, tariff and custom compliance.
- 49 per cent outsourced freight auditing services.
- 48 per cent outsourced warehousing.

Backing up that KPMG-Peat Marwick study is a 1995 finding by trucking firm Ryder of 1300 executives that showed '80 per cent of executives now believe that product delivery is now as important as product quality'. In information technology (IT), the Outsourcing Institute's own study together with Frost & Sullivan Market Intelligence showed that:

- 50 per cent of all companies with IT budgets in excess of $5 million are either outsourcing or actively considering it.
- 85 per cent of banking and finance companies with IT budgets in excess of $5 million are either outsourcing or are actively considering it.
- By the end of 1995, one in every $12 spent in corporate America on IT will flow through an outsourcing contract

Outsourcing

(today other studies have hiked that number upwards).

■ By the end of 1995, over $38 billion will be spent in corporate America on IT outsourcing (again other studies raise that number).

In human resources (HR) a 1994 study of 400 companies by the Olsten Corporation found:

■ 45 per cent of the executives surveyed said they outsourced payroll management.
■ 38 per cent said they outsourced tax management.
■ 35 per cent said they outsourced benefits management.
■ 34 per cent said they outsourced worker compensation.
■ The number of HR executives using outsourcing as part of a flexible staffing strategy increased from 18 per cent to 30 per cent in just one year.

A parallel study (referred to earlier) by The Conference Board added to the HR picture:

■ 85 per cent of the executives surveyed had personal experience with leading an outsourcing effort.
■ 67 per cent of the pension departments studied outsourced at least one function.

In health care – an area coming under the full glare of the spotlight across social security-bound Europe – the 1995 annual survey by the US Hospitals & Health Network discovered that:

■ 67 per cent of hospitals use outsourcing providers for at least one department within their operations.
■ 90 per cent of these hospitals use outsourcing providers for support services, 77 per cent for clinical services and 51 per cent for business services.

The list can go on and on; it is virtually endless. What this shows is not just sets of statistics, but the extent to which outsourcing has taken over the business of doing business. Vilified it may be by some, who see it as yet another departure from the way we used to do business, but it is not something new, it is entrenched in the way all of us are doing our business today – to a greater of a lesser extent.

In search of the source

However, before we all get too euphoric about outsourcing, we need to take a quick look at some of the problems. Outsourcing may be a key part – in some cases most – of the way to new business success. It may also be changing quickly into a strategic weapon rather that a quick-fix way to cut costs. But it is also being increasingly recognized that many early outsourcing deals were poorly planned and companies have been reaping a sad harvest.

Don't confuse outsourcing with cost-cutting. Chances are it won't work for long and you'll lose out big!

Alan Cane's article in the *Financial Times* notes that 'critics maintain, however, that outsourcing contracts frequently favour the vendor and that savings are hard to identify'. It goes on to add, 'the biggest problem with most outsourcing contracts is unanticipated costs. In one example, a petrol company was charged almost $500 000 in excess fees in the first month of a new contract.'

An April 1996 article in *Business Week*, supports the view that some contracts have gone bad. 'Some companies,' it reported, 'have found themselves locked into long-term contracts with outside suppliers that are no longer competitive,' and adds that others, 'have outsourced so much staff that they have no choice but to bring in consultants to evaluate and renegotiate deals gone bad.'

Articles in the business press criticizing wholesale outsourcing all focus on the same thing. What looks good today may be insanity tomorrow. Many reports cite cases where failure to take account of the longer term has meant paying through the nose for less than good-value services.

The lesson here – and stressed throughout the book – is think ahead, don't sign exclusivity agreements without considering the longer-term implications. Don't get stuck paying today's market price when a technological breakthrough could slash costs a year or two years down the road. In most businesses margins are tight anyway, creating that kind of problem for your business can be suicidal. It is ironic to see – but sadly true – that some corporations have collapsed through paying out unrealistic amounts to outsourcers who two or three years earlier were hailed as the saviours of the business.

Let's just agree that outsourcing is something that we are all going to have to examine closely. Far from being a trend in big business, it affects everyone, the industrial giants, small and medium enterprises (SMEs) and the euphemistically termed mom-and-pop operations. The other point to consider is that outsourcing for all these categories is not just something you do as a giver of work to others, it can quite easily be the other way around, being an outsource provider to others. In fact some corporations are doing very well with a mixture of both – acting as an outsource provider to clients as one part of their business and outsourcing non-core activity at the other end.

Don't sign up with a consultant who treats outsourcing as the flavour of the month. Look for a specialist firm that has experience.

Whether you are a senior, middle ranked or junior executive in a corporation, a partner in a start-up or an entrepreneur, outsourcing is already affecting the way you do business – the way you work. Chances are that the effect is going to increase and multiply. The trick is to ride the wave of change, not get knocked over by it.

As we will see in the next chapter there are a lot of reasons for doing it, which one's you choose depend on your business and where you want to take it.

The outsourcing story in three minutes

Don't have time to read all the way through this book? Then whatever else you miss out, don't miss reading this box. In the research for this book I carried out an interview with Michael Corbett of the New York-based Outsourcing Institute. Widely accepted as the senior organization world-wide for the study of outsourcing and its leading champion, the Outsourcing Institute believes that the process – properly and professionally applied – can only be beneficial to today's business, and is a great deal more than a cost-cutting excercise.

Michael Corbett's views on outsourcing as a strategic tool for today's business provide a useful and practical insight into this phenomenon that is taking more and more of our attention as managers.

1 *How would you best describe outsourcing within the operations of an organization?* **Outsourcing (or sourcing) is simply the 'make versus buy' decision organizations have always had to make. What has changed is that the number and capability of external suppliers has exploded. They offer specialized solutions for every con-**

ceivable aspect of a company's operations. Additionally, technology has made it easier than ever to integrate the operations of separate companies into a cohesive whole. Finally, competition – relentless and global – has forced every organization to re-examine and challenge every aspect of its operations. In the light of these different dynamics, outsourcing becomes the very critical, very strategic process of examining the organization's value chain, understanding its core competencies and making smart, strategic decisions for sourcing everything else from the best-in-the-world source – be it external or internal.

2 *Typically, who in the organization should be responsible for outsourcing?* Outsourcing is a strategic tool for organizational change which, to be effective, must be driven from the very top of the organization. In most organizations we see the initial effort driven by a 'team' commissioned by senior management: this team is typically cross-functional and cross-disciplinary. Made up of line executives, purchasing, finance, human resources, legal, communications, the team is charged with the mission I outlined in question 1. Out of this initial effort, we are more frequently seeing the creation of a position dedicated to the continuation of the process and acting as the repository of organizational expertise on outsourcing. Although we haven't seen a Chief Resource Officer yet, there are many examples of Director of Outsourcing and Strategic Sourcing Managers.

3 *Is outsourcing something the CEO needs to champion?* Outsourcing has to be driven from the top of the organization. It implies fundamental changes in strategy, organization and people that can only be sustained by a top-of-the-organization mandate. On a practical level, however, CEOs don't stay close to the details of implementation. They commission and champion the effort, challenge those involved and endorse and help communicate the results.

4 *Where has outsourcing – so far – achieved its greatest successes?* Obviously the more tactical benefits are easier to measure and achieve. Typically companies report a nine per cent reduction in operating costs and a 15 per cent improvement in capacity and quality in out-

Outsourcing

sourced functions. Strategically, many large and successful companies have made outsourcing a key part of their business strategy – Microsoft, GE and Chrysler are all good examples.

5 *What about the downside of outsourcing?* The least success is found in cases where financial savings have driven the transaction too hard. Savings can, obviously, be achieved by doing the job cheaper, paying people less, cutting back on quality, but this short-term approach can backfire as internal and external customers begin to see poor service. Lots of examples can be found in the press of these 'failures.' They are a story that loves to get told. As for areas or industries, the one common thread right now in the USA at least is unionized companies and crafts. Frequently outsourcing of manufacturing is to non-unionized companies and this has led in some cases to management/labour strife. We've had some well-publicized strikes over outsourcing including GM, Boeing and McDonnell-Douglas.

6 *Do you think that outsourcing is a U.S. led phenomenon?* Yes. In the first place in the U.S. we were required to make the most fundamental changes as the impact of the global economy hit us, forcing the last recession. Just think of our auto industry in the 1970s and 1980s, or IBM in the late 1980s and early 1990s and you'll see what I mean. Second, the US economy I suspect is more service based than any other. About 80 percent of our employment is in service companies. As a result, the number and capability of outsourcing service providers based in the USA is amazing. Just think of EDS, ISSC, Johnson Controls, Pitney-Bowes, UPS, the Big-six accounting firms all operating globally and carrying this structural business approach with them.

7 *There is considerable outsourcing advice available from consulting firms, what do you think of the quality of their advice?* Businesses adopting outsourcing as a new business model and management tool can certainly benefit from the experiences of other firms and the expertise of proven practitioners. My one caution is that general management consulting firms can approach outsourcing as the 'management fad of the month' and be

too general in their approach to the topic. In this case they are not offering much value. Outsourcing is a very specialized discipline, which argues for working with organizations that have dedicated themselves to the topic – continuously expanding their knowledge and skill.

8 *Do you think that some corporations have gone too far and off-loaded too much?* There are always arguments to this effect – I even joke of some-day starting the Insourcing Institute! But seriously, no. The key issue, the thing to remember at all times, is to hold the organization's core competencies close and then carefully and strategically (emphasis on those two words) make the right decisions for all other aspects of the operation. Neither do I see a reverse trend. What I would expect is a continual refinement of the relationships, which would result in continual movement of selected activities from outside-to-in and inside-to-out. At times I am certain that some of this will be picked up and reported as a reversal in the trend, but I doubt it will actually be one.

Executive summary

- Business life today is just too complicated to do everything in-house.

- Outsourcing isn't new, it's just the emphasis on it that's changed how we think about it.

- Outsourcing is being seen less and less as a tactical, cost-saving drive and more and more as a strategic direction that the organization follows.

- Outsourcing goes under a lot of different disguises. Make sure you and your suppliers are talking the same language from the beginning.

- Don't confuse outsourcing with cost-cutting. Chances are it won't work for long.

Outsourcing

- ■ **Never sign an outsourcing agreement without considering carefully the longer-term implications.**

- ■ **Don't sign up with a consultant who treats outsourcing as the flavour of the month, the new trend. Look for a specialist.**

2

Outsourcing at the core of your business

Looking at outsourcing today there is – if we want to be true to ourselves – a definite dichotomy. On the one hand, we are saying outsource all the things that we don't do well, that don't give us a competitive advantage, that are not unique to our company, that don't give away the secrets of our success. On the other hand, however, what we are saying is hold on to the core business, the competencies that we, and we alone, do well. But if outsourcing is to become a strategic issue, rather than just a tactical, quick trip to get some cash in the system – the corporate equivalent of a bank robbery – surely it then becomes one of our core abilities. The ability to outsource well. To follow the success guidelines, not to foolishly embark on the outsourcing journey without proper preparation, must become a core competence.

So it might help for us to consider outsourcing not just in the two ways we examined in Chapter 1 (as a socio-economic phenomenon with the attendant ramifications for workforces the world over) or as a simple management-driven action to keep the corporate ship afloat in the short or medium term), but to divide it into:

Outsourcing

■ The tactical, cost-driven view
■ The strategic, organization-driven view

There are now clearly two levels of outsourcing – tactical (short-term, results-driven) and strategic (long-term, process-driven). Make sure you know which you are doing.

First, let us take a look at those who believe – and in many cases of outsourcing experience they are right – that cost is the driver: whether bringing down prices, slashing headcount or any other urgent imperative. A recent study by Luk Van Wassenhove, Professor of Operations Management and Operations Research at INSEAD, the European business school, headlined cost as the outsourcing driver. Says the report, 'When asked what was the most important reason for deciding to utilize third party logistics providers [outsourcers], most managers indicated cost reduction now and in the future.' The report goes on, 'executives stated that the use of third party logistic providers would alter the financial structure of their firm by "making fixed costs variable" and "reducing capital investment".' Later, the study says, 'The current trend toward "lean and mean" organizations is apparent in the majority of responses. Many of the respondents believe that third parties can do things more efficiently and effectively than when done in-house. Using third party companies provides a manufacturer, according to one manager, with "the ability to choose companies who have proven track records in logistics, at costs in keeping with product profiles". Other respondents contended that third parties could offer better quality and service due to their special expertise, professionalism and qualified personnel.'

The constant search for lean and mean is sure, but inherent in that part of the INSEAD report is a definite feeling that companies are doing it because others are already ahead, that perhaps some are getting into it in that classic knee-jerk reaction referred to in Chapter 1. When that happens people and businesses can get hurt.

The INSEAD study's findings are amply supported by Paul Strassman, author of *The Politics of Information Management: Policy Guidelines*, The Information Economics Press, 1995, in an article in the UK publication *Computer World*. Entitled, Outsourcing: a game for loser's, Strassmann's article begins 'Strategy isn't driving outsourcing. Statistics show the real reason companies outsource is simple – they're in financial trouble.' After presenting a series of statistics that show companies in trouble turning to outsourcing like a drunk to a barroom, Strassmann concludes, 'Outsourcing is, in reality, only

Outsourcing at the core of your business

one aspect of a currently popular downsizing trend among troubled corporations. It is executed under another label, just as re-engineering is a euphemism for cut-back in most cases.' He adds, 'I am in favour of outsourcing for any of the good reasons that would take advantage of somebody else's capacity to accumulate know-how faster than if it remains home-grown. It should not be applied as an emetic.'

Comments Brenda Vathauer of a Hewlett-Packard division in the USA in an article in *Information Week*, 'We've seen a greater openness to outsourcing in the last 12 months. Prior to that, outsourcing was a dirty word. Companies typically outsourced when they hit financial difficulties and needed a quick transfer of assets – and a cash infusion.'

Many organizations are still using short-term outsourcing techniques as knee-jerk, 'we're in trouble' cost-cutting exercises. If you are doing that make sure you know why.

A 1995 Outsourcing Institute survey, *Purchasing Dynamics, Expectations and Outcomes*, reported 'an overemphasis on short-term benefits as the reasons for out-sourcing.' The report added, 'we believe that the problem comes about when the strategic reasons for outsourcing are overshadowed by the need to address a short-term business issue. This does not, of course, mean that outsourcing cannot be used as a tool to solve short-term problems, it just suggests that there may be trade-offs in these situations and that the longer-term return can get compromised.'

In Brenda Vathauer's *Information Week* article, Adrian Holcombe, director of network services at Ascom Timeplex in the UK warned 'never outsource what you don't understand. The goal is to outsource the things you *can* do, but would rather not.'

Never outsource what you don't understand. Outsource things you *can* do, but would rather not – that way you keep control.

In a recent study specific to the outsourcing of Data Centres, consulting firm Deloitte & Touche reported that 'cost reduction is commonly perceived as the primary driver for outsourcing.' However, their study showed that vendor expertise was rated slightly higher than pure price. The study also showed that respondents' expectations in overall cost reductions and reductions of capital were in the main fully realized.

Venture capital group 3I asked UK based financial directors for their views on outsourcing in a 1994 study, entitled *plc UK – a Focus on Corporate Trends* (Figure 2.1). According to their report, 'the majority of respondents who had outsourced in the previous five years mentioned cost reduction as a reason. Taking advantage of expertise not available in-house was also a popular reason, and often both (to reduce costs and improve

Outsourcing

efficiency). The notion of "concentrating on what we do well" was widespread. One respondent said that outsourcing would, "avoid training and career-path issues with specialist staff". Interestingly, one respondent said the motive was to "define costs", i.e. to improve his information about the business.'

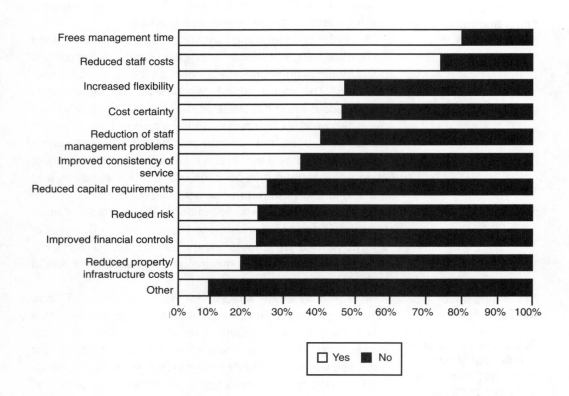

Figure 2.1 The main benefits of the outsourcing undertaken. (*Source*: 3I – *A Focus on Corporate Trends*, UK plc, 1994)

Getting motivated to outsource

A 1993 study by Andersen Consulting across the UK concluded 'The primary, current motivation for considering outsourcing is cost, which – when taken with better value for money – accounts for 70 per cent of respondents' main reasoning. Their key findings are outlined in Table 2.1

Table 2.1 Motivation for considering outsourcing

Factor	All reasons	Main reason
Reduced costs	70	51
Better value for money	30	19
Improved quality of service	23	3
Expertise	31	8
Reduced management structure	12	3
Increased flexibility	11	1
Government White Paper	5	1
Improve efficiency	4	2
Focus on core processes	4	2
Lack of resource/start-up	3	1
Other	19	9

Source: *A Study on Outsourcing*, Andersen Consulting, 1993

Even back in 1993 Andersen Consulting with that study were quick to see that while many were using outsourcing and its derivatives as a brutal cost-cutting process there was another side to the outsource equation. In their introduction to the study they pointed out 'What has emerged is that there are clearly two levels of approach to outsourcing. The first uses outsourcing as "contracting out", to achieve tactical benefits in the generally accepted way. This seems to represent the bulk of an established marketplace.' But Andersen added 'The second approach appears to be founded on a fundamental reappraisal of the business model and modes of operation that a company uses. In this approach, external parties are brought in (rather than pieces of the business being disposed of) as part of a structural change in that business model.' They concluded 'Given this, there are clearly more issues to be dealt with (beneath the overall umbrella of outsourcing) than have been recognized so far. There is not one marketplace, with its own trends,

Outsourcing

drivers and motivators, but several at various stages of development. The challenge for us all is evident.' Andersen Consulting followed up their landmark survey in 1994 and concluded, 'Cost reduction remains the primary reason for outsourcing. However, increasing importance is being placed on improved service, access to expertise, the ability to focus management time on core processes and greater flexibility.'

Outsourcing isn't about cost savings, it's about more effective performance in the longer term.

Even in the pure IT business, studies have been starting to show some changes in attitude to outsourcing. An International Data Corporation study, *Business Strategies for Outsourcing*, commented, 'Originally, IT outsourcing was little more than "box minding" for a fee,' but no longer. 'The marketplace has matured very rapidly in recent years and customers have become far more sophisticated in the scope and complexity of their requirements. There is now a growing acceptance that outsourcing can be used not just to cut costs – in fact that may not be the aim of the exercise at all – but as a means to raise the level of IT delivery and generally make IT far more responsive, if not pre-emptive, to the needs of business.' The study adds, 'This change in attitude has encouraged new players to enter the IT marketplace with innovative service offerings that go beyond the traditional facilities management and in some cases into the very heart of the customer's business.'

KPMG guidelines for outsourcing

The KPMG Impact Programme is a partnership of major user organizations in the UK that have been working together since 1989. In 1995 they published – through their Outsourcing Working Group – a set of guidelines for potential outsourcers. Entitled *Best Practice Guidelines for Outsourcing*, it lists the key management, HR, service and communication issues. While not exhaustive, it does provide some initial insights into the complexities of embarking on an outsourcing process and serves as a useful *aide-mémoire*. Consider how many of these you have examined, how many you've glossed over and how many you never even considered:

Outsourcing at the core of your business

Management issues

- Retain in-house control over strategic direction
- Retain responsibility for setting standards to which the supplier must conform
- Use a prime contractor
- Make the supplier responsible for delivery
- Be prescriptive about the service requirements rather than the method of service delivery
- Never lose sight of the business-driven objectives of outsourcing
- Avoid lock-in to any single supplier
- Expect value-for-money, but accept the supplier's need to make a profit – a partnership
- Understand the strategic, political and managerial implications of the scope of your outsourcing
- Define the supplier's points of contact – ensure adherence
- Have an appropriate person to manage the contract
- Keep the procedures simple
- Regularly review the outsourcing contract and relationship with the supplier
- *Never* stop negotiating
- Re-tender contracts at defined intervals
- Regularly review the outsourcing market to identify trends and changes
- Monitor supplier's resource levels and business knowledge
- Encourage cooperative contract evolution and take advantage of developing technologies
- Retain and exercise the right to conduct IS audits at the supplier's premises
- Aim for continuous improvement

HR issues

- Ensure sufficient number and quality of in-house staff remain to manage the outsourced situation
- Promote a continuing bond between supplier staff and end-users
- Make the morale of supplier staff a customer concern

Outsourcing

- Sort out personality conflicts as soon as possible
- Review regularly in-house staff skills and numbers
- Involve end-users in monitoring service delivery against targets
- Retain the right to veto supplier's choice of key staff

Service/business issues

- Match expectations with needs, not historical achievements
- Have a contingency escape plan covering the outsourcing contract, software ownership, etc.
- Maintain the right to invite tenders for new work
- Recognize that requirements will change and be willing to adjust costs accordingly
- Ensure that service level agreements are always realistic and do not expect them to remain static
- Continue to benchmark the service and consider alternative approaches
- Discuss with all concerned, at the earliest possible stage, plans which could affect services

Communications/understanding issues

- Clearly define the scope and interface of what is outsourced
- Establish unambiguous roles and responsibilities for the customer, end-user and supplier
- Maintain regular customer/supplier contact at various levels – even when things are going well
- Establish an open relationship, be prepared to compromise
- Build a relationship of trust with the supplier
- Hold regular meetings to monitor achievements
- Define clear escalation procedures
- Do not abuse escalation procedures – nit-picking with managers is counterproductive
- Encourage the supplier to propose changes based on their expertise
- Ensure customer awareness, understanding and commitment.

Outsourcing at the core of your business

Using or adapting this checklist, fleshing it out to meet you own specific needs as well as sharing it with others can only contribute to the overall success of the outsourcing process. Each of the issues are explained in detail in *Best Practices Guidelines* under the headings Explanation, Benefits, Risks and Suggestions. Further information is given at the end of the book.

The second age of outsourcing

Andersen Consulting's contention that outsourcing was not just a chop-chop, pass-on-your-problems phenomenon but had deeper, more fundamental corporate issues inherent in it – the two-way split between tactical and strategic outsourcing – was borne out by findings of another study by the PA Consulting Group in 1996. Boldly going perhaps a little further than any other outsourcing promoter had gone before, their introduction to their survey *International Strategic Sourcing* says, 'We conclude from our research that outsourcing is here to stay; it constitutes a genuinely new approach to business.' PA Consulting go on to suggest that 'it is not driven primarily by costs or by government pressure. Instead it is a fundamental part of the universal search for more effective performance.' Concluding that outsourcing is indeed – for those that want or can use it that way – a core part of a business, they add, 'Organizations that aspire to be world-class in their own markets recognize they themselves cannot be world-class at everything. Yet only by gaining access to world-class services in all areas that are significant to their future business can they achieve the vital combination of quality and efficiency necessary for success.'

It would appear that outsourcing well, outsourcing professionally is going to be a unique competence for many in the future and one that will both define and assure their success. Others with less drive and imagination will still see it as a part of the downsizing process. Instead of using it to energize their organizations they will use it simply as a tool to trim off the bits and pieces they think they don't want.

in brief

'Outsourcing is not a quick fix to a badly managed process. There is no reason to believe someone else will fix a problem overnight that a company has failed to manage.' – **Lawrence Beuttner, senior vice-president, First Chicago**

PA Consulting's findings are so revealing about the second age of outsourcing that it is worth looking at them in greater detail. The management summary of their findings continues throughout to underscore their belief that outsourcing is a significant part of long-term management strategy. Here's their view. 'Outsourcing is now a significant element in the business planning of most major organizations, both public and private. Increasingly, activities that do not form part of a company's competitive positioning are outsourced to others who are seen to be able to do them better.' The report continues, 'Although most organizations are satisfied with their outsourcing, only a few are achieving the levels of benefit that are potentially available. Given that many are planning to outsource more, they risk failing to win proper returns on their investment time and effort.' PA explain why. 'Outsourcing is not driven primarily by cost or by external pressure. It is a fundamental part of the universal search for more effective performance. The nature of this extended outsourcing will also take it, progressively, into more complex areas – into more challenging functions, into whole business processes and into a global dimension.' While noting that the most frequently outsourced services are property services, catering and IT, PA's report conjures up a new organizational dimension for outsourcing as a management process. 'There are clear signs,' they say, 'that outsourcing is moving toward the centre of organizations,' and this 'pattern of outsourcing growth is repeated internationally.'

C. Stephen Carr, the president of IPT, a new product development firm in Palo Alto, says the first mistake that many executives make is that old cost-cutting approach, 'viewing outsourcing as a reactive technique, placing the emphasis on financial analysis of direct costs, overhead, working capital and profits'. He points out that 'Often these financial issues are considered incrementally without further thought to building and sustaining a competitive advantage over a significant period of time.' Carr's view is that what he calls an 'assertive outsourcing strategy, provides benefits from outsourcing by learning not only the potential learning by the supplier, but the potential learning from the supplier'. He lists the potential benefits from building a two-way programme – part of understanding the outsourcing process as a core part of your business strategy as :

- Improved time to market
- Improved competitiveness
- Reduced capital investment
- Reduced costs
- Increased revenue per employee
- Improved operating efficiencies
- Improved management
- Reduced risks

More than just a relationship

While much of Carr's list is the same as those who are motivated by the 'cut the costs at all costs' brigade, he and others see it differently. Being skilled at building relationships that work in the longer term, learning from each other and above all managing and keeping control of the process are the keys, not a quick cutting of operational costs.

Control, control, control – that's a central outsourcing issue that too many forget.

But it is more than just building a relationship. Michael Corbett of the Outsourcing Institute has some excellent examples of those corporations going the extra mile for each other and integrating their operations to make it all work. Says Corbett, 'We've found that leaders in the outsourcing revolution are doing more than what is called for in the structure of the relationship – the most successful forms of outsourcing go well beyond the structure of the agreement. Generally these relationships fall into four categories :

Outsourcing

- Integrating operations
- Mastering change
- Providing cutting-edge business solutions
- Sharing risks and rewards'

Using the experience of the Outsourcing Institute, Corbett is able to offer examples that fit these categories. 'In the area of integrated operations, there is a law firm in Chicago (Bates, Mecler, Bolger and Tilson) who were able to triple their operation in 18 months. One of the ways they were able to do that was by creating integrated operational relationships through outsourcing contracts. For example, they have one with Arthur Andersen, who provide a controller function, billing function, payroll, overseeing payroll and doing payables. Having access to people with great familiarity with their area of expertise is one of the things which has enabled them to achieve that – to integrate their operation with other organizations.' 'An example of mastering change,' says Corbett, 'is Circle K and Unisys. Circle K is the largest operator of company-owned convenience stores in the USA and the largest independent petrol retailer in the world. Obviously technology is changing their business, and mastering that is critical to them. They ended up looking to Unisys to do two things. To stabilize their operation and to provide an aggressive migration to new technology. Their chief information officer says that they see their partner as an extension of their business – leading their efforts to better harness technology.'

Michael Corbett chooses automaker Chrysler for an example of cutting-edge business solutions. 'Chrysler, for those not aware of it, has actually got to the point where 70 per cent of the supply of parts and components is being manufactured by outside organizations. In fact all the US automobile manufacturers are moving in the same direction – which is still short of the Japanese who are running at about 75 per cent on average.' He continues, 'These relationships with suppliers involve far more than just manufacturing. What Chrysler is now looking for is for the suppliers to design, engineer and manufacture the sub-components that are coming into their products. In fact, in one of their newest models, the interior of the car is four separate sub-assemblies that come from four individual providers. But they also use Ryder [the trucking firm] for in-bound logistics

Outsourcing at the core of your business

As organizations become more process driven, outsourcing is a natural fit with new business structures and it forces businesses to define their core competencies.

at all of their mini-van plants, and MCI for networking. They are looking to get, what they call, the one-day mini-van, where the customer can order a mini-van in the morning and it will roll off the assembly line at the end of the day. To do that you need incredible networking between the company, its assembly plants, its suppliers and its dealers. In the area of shared risks we are seeing growing cases where out-sourcing vendors are being measured and rewarded by the bottom-line business benefit they are bringing to the rela-tionship. For example, they are being tied to the final output of the assembly plant, or they are actually making invest-ments and sharing the risks and the rewards of those invest-ments.'

All these examples show that corporations – perhaps more so in the USA than anywhere else right now – are using outsourcing to examine their organization from the ground up. The businesses quoted by Michael Corbett are all in out-sourcing for the duration. It's not a one-time hit but an endless process, that they hope they can continue to improve upon.

As many are beginning to realize, this two-way split that outsourcing is undergoing can be looked at in yet another way. Outsourcing can be used as a means to an end, a fast and furious way to simply shake costs and other elements out of a system. But as it is embraced in a more strategic way by some, it can be seen as a never-ending process. It becomes an integral part of how you manage.

Interviews and research for this book continually referred to re-engineering's disasters – where executives confused the ongoing change process that it advocates with quick-fix downsizing. Downsizing was only the first part (where it was needed) of the re-engineering process. But many never got any further.

There seems little doubt that outsourcing is the same. Lumped together with downsizing as a cost-cutting, people-cutting solution, it has not had the opportunity to show what it can really do when properly applied. Outsourcing is one element that can come out of and remain a part of the re-engineered organization to a greater or lesser degree. But it is certainly an important part of the new-look organizational structure – ignore it at your peril. On the other side of the coin, of course, are the tremendous benefits to be had being an outsourcing vendor.

It's a big market out there – get to know it

Whichever side of the outsourcing divide you are on, giver or taker of work – you can be on both quite easily – there's going to be a lot of pie to cut up. International Data Corporation have estimated the total global outsourcing market as exceeding $120 billion by the end of the century – just three years away. Already estimates say that we have passed $70 billion annually. Information Services provider Dun and Bradstreet (D&B) say that 146 000 outsourcing companies are listed as doing business with more than 1.6 million firms in the D&B information base. 'The industry most frequently using an outsourcing company is the business service sector,' they say, 'followed by the retail trade, wholesalers and manufacturers.'

However, in these US-based statistics outsourcing is certainly ruled by the mom-and-pop operators, 'Companies providing outsourcing services tend to have relatively small dollar sales,' say D&B, 'more than 52 per cent of the companies are reporting sales volume of sales less than $500 000.'

However, times seem set to get tougher for the smaller operator. According to a study by Penton Research Services, although 44 per cent of purchasing decision makers said they had increased outsourcing over the last five years, 'larger organizations provide the greatest sales opportunities for suppliers, but are getting tougher to sell to. Over the last five years, 60 per cent of the large organizations have increased the amount of outsourcing done, while reducing the number of vendors bought from.'

What's getting outsourced?

So what is getting outsourced? A study by Arthur Andersen and the Economist Intelligence Unit among financial managers on what typically gets outsourced from an organizational point of view, showed a huge range from legal services and payroll to training and fleet management. INSEAD's study of logistic services quotes everything from warehouse management and order fulfilment to product assembly and spare part support. Andersen Consulting's

Outsourcing at the core of your business

study showed that more than a quarter of those surveyed currently outsource:

- Recruitment
- IT
- Training
- Pensions administration
- Payroll
- Building management
- Fleet management
- Estate management
- Credit card processing

Up and coming areas include maintenance management, warehousing, engineering and design, marketing.

It would seem that depending on your business focus, you can outsource just about anything. You are only limited by your imagination and, of course, your need to hold on to what makes your business unique. A good example of that is given by Jerry Mirelli, executive vice-president of New Jersey-based Technology and Business Integrators (TBI). 'You never outsource your secret formula,' he advises, 'Coca-Cola will always keep theirs internal.' Mirelli goes on to the difficult part, 'The challenge is deciding what your secret is!' then adds, 'For instance, Nike doesn't actually manufacture their sneakers. This would be a mistake if Nike defined itself as a sneaker manufacturer, but since it defines itself as a sneaker marketing and design company, it doesn't pose a problem.' Continues Mirelli, 'You can bet that they still manage the manufacturer, however, since no company should outsource the management of the enterprise.'

Outsourcing gives managers time to concentrate on the things they do well – don't confuse it with getting rid of the things you don't like.

Peter Warner, sourcing director for Nike's Apparel Division in Europe, agrees with Mirelli's view of the company, 'Yes, the idea and concept of outsourcing is somewhat part of the basis on which Nike is founded,' he says, 'that is, to design, develop and produce high-quality shoes and apparel for championship athletes. This could only be accomplished by producing them at a lower price in foreign markets and exporting them back to the US.' Warner, who says he is speaking from a knowledge of the clothing side of the business only, says that there are three areas where Nike outsources:

Outsourcing

- Garment manufacturing
- Fabric or other materials development
- Research and design on specific items such as new fabrics

Acknowledging that Nike has come in for some serious criticism – especially in the USA for some of its outsourcing decisions, notably to some suppliers in the Third World – Peter Warner says that it isn't correct that the company outsources solely on the basis of where they can find the lowest cost production. 'Right now everyone would assume that Asia and the cheap countries we have out there are the best areas,' he says, 'but this is not necessarily true.' Warner explains that 'for example, we produce 50 per cent of our apparel for the European market, right here in Europe. So it is not necessarily the cheapest place or price, but rather where we can get the best quality, delivery and a fair price. Indeed, Nike apparel is produced in 150 factories in places all over the world – Asia, Western and Eastern Europe, Latin America and the US just to name a few.'

Whatever your views on Nike and other similar manufacturers, they certainly know how to build an organization based on keeping the core idea and 'secrets' to themselves and getting everything else done outside. While this may be a lot further than many existing businesses, not built to do this from the outset, might want to go, the lessons that they have learned and the example that they provide bears watching, not just now but in the future.

Outsourcers are everywhere

While it is easier to start from scratch, you can change your culture if you know why you are doing it and know what you want.

Elsewhere, great outsourcers abound. Coca-Cola, cited by Jerry Minelli, and its arch-rival Pepsi license bottlers but control marketing. DHL, Fedex and UPS are locking horns and chasing major corporate logistics work, not one-off packages around the globe. McDonald's, Pizza Hut and other fast-food operators have learned how to leverage the name but outsource much of what they do in support services. Giant facilities management operations like Johnson Controls and ISS have sprung up from contract cleaners to total estate managers.

Outsourcing at the core of your business

Here are a few more examples of what the big, diverse world of outsourcing is offering:

■ In 1995 Xerox agreed to pay over $3 billion to EDS to manage most of its computer operations around the globe. The deal is part of a massive re-engineering process designed to save $1 million a day. Reason? Xerox, like others, needs someone in the know to keep up with the IT boom.

■ IBM has turned over the running of its building facilities in Europe, the Middle East and Africa to Johnson Controls. The multi-million dollar contract gives Johnson Controls the management of more than 20 million square feet of facilities in thirteen countries.

■ Johnson Controls is everywhere. In head-to-head competition with Lear they control about half the production of car seats in North America and Europe. Counting seats made by outside companies, the figure climbs to 70 per cent.

■ Catering giants Sodexo and Gardner Merchant from France and the UK merged to create the world's largest contract catering group.

■ Hilton Hotels teamed up with Litton Computer Services to develop a totally new database and data communications system, allowing Hilton to steal a march on competitors by being able to predict more accurately best prices up to a year in advance.

■ AT&T Solutions which provides technology lifecycle management has joined with CSX Transportation which manages a rail network of 19 000 miles of track to ensure consistently efficient telecommunications.

■ Whitbread, the UK brewing and beverage group, signed a multi-million dollar deal to outsource the systems development and maintenance of its IT functions.

■ Even the world's favourite airline, British Airways – long perceived as a holdout in doing everything in-house – is

Outsourcing

being swayed and is spinning off its much-admired maintenance services division and outsourcing from it as well. Ticketing, check-in and baggage handling.

Don't think traditional. Think about what you'd like to be as an organization, then try to achieve it. It takes belief in yourselves that you can make it work.

■ Digital Equipment linked up with Kodak Imaging Services to design, implement, and operate print-on-demand centres.

■ Typhoon Software of Santa Barbara, California, has set itself up to be a true low-cost provider of computer solutions. All its programmers and technicians are Russian and located in St Petersburg. Latest technology ensures compatability, security and speed.

■ EML (Expatriate Management Limited) is building a reputation from its London base for outsourcing expatriate employees, taking the strain off hard-pressed and often ill-qualified HR departments.

■ Saks Fifth Avenue invited Deloitte & Touche to sit on their Profit Improvement Committee, which resulted in outsourcing its internal audit operations and credit department processing.

■ Back in 1991 BP Exploration set a new outsourcing standard by contracting out its accounting function and staff plus the IT support groups.

Define your outsourcing requirements in clear, complete and measurable terms and stick with them – you'll be glad you did.

■ Ryder Dedicated Logistics designed from the ground up a dynamic distribution system to keep pace with the galloping growth of Papa Johnas – the fastest-growing pizza chain in the USA. This included training drivers to handle the cargo properly and realize that they as Ryder employees often had more interface with the store owner. Their opinion of the driver quickly becomes their attitude toward Papa Johnas.

■ Canon offers its customers two repair programmes. But once Canon takes the call it is actually the Cerplex Group that delivers the service through a carefully integrated programme – that leaves the happy customer none the wiser.

Outsourcing at the core of your business

■ Avis Rent-A-Car has been able to stay up to the minute in technology due to its twenty year outsourcing deal with Automatic Data Processing, who have become an ever more integral part of the Avis business. In fact ADP is a major outsource vendor, handling the payroll of more than 17 million workers at over 300 000 client companies.

■ Chi-Chi's International (CCI), headquartered in Brussels, Belgium and with its Mexican Dinner House restaurants in twelve countries from Indonesia, the Middle East and Europe outsources everything to long-time partners. Eat a chicken fajita in Bali, Kuwait or London and it comes from the same producer in France, same weight, same spices, same quality – they even source the sauce!

■ Hooker Cockram, an Australia-based construction company, took itself back to the drawing board and rebuilt itself. Instead of doing everything they out-sourced everything from plans to payroll, even the con-struction staff, concentrating on their core ability of getting business.

■ Barclays Bank – one of Britain's biggest high street banks – put its computer operations out to tender, but let its in-house team put in a bid. Theirs won. Not only did they stay, but they have since won outsourced business from a major utility, a merchant bank and others. Part of that came from the realization that computing for them was a core activity.

■ Group 4 – one of Europe's leading security management organizations – made headlines when it won the first out-sourced contract from Her Majesty's Prison Service for the remand and transfer of prisoners around Britain. After a few weeks of horror publicity about escaped convicts, they quickly settled down to a routine that has had few glitches in recent years.

Look for outsourcers with whom you have a cultural fit – who regard their business the way you do your own.

■ Many contend that outsourcing is new but UK-based apparel retailer Marks & Spencer have been doing it for almost a generation and following the rules – or perhaps

Outsourcing

making them. Close supervision, an obsession with quality and a strong value-for-money image led them out of simple clothes retailing into other success areas like prepared food.

■ Faced with massive social costs that were making it one of the cuckoos of an already sick industry, the Belgian state airline Sabena, outsourced many of its regional air links to small start-ups and charter companies. While frowned on by the company's air and ground crews they have so far got away with it, largely due to the threat of greater job losses if their plan to cut costs didn't work.

■ DHL, the express delivery service, with headquarters in Brussels, has become a dynamic insourcer and outsourcer. On one side it is gleaning major contracts as a supplier of total logistic solutions for major corporations, on the other it has freed up capital by outsourcing street deliveries to independent drivers.

Certainly, based on this sort of record, this trend is unlikely to reverse. And while shaking out fixed costs inside an organization seems to dominate for the present, the saving in management time is seen as an increasingly major factor. What that translates into is giving management time to concentrate on the things it does best – not the things it has to do. Properly managed it sounds like an almost perfect world. The old Protestant work ethic always suggested that part of earning your living was the ability to buckle down and do the things that had to be done, even if you didn't like them. Today, there's a new game in town. If you don't like to do it, you don't have to plod through it anymore – hating every minute. You can get someone else (who actually likes it, by the way!) to do it instead. If it saves you money and improves overall productivity as well – why not?

in brief

'Outsourcing is not an end result in itself. It is simply a tool that you are using to achieve organizational objectives ...' – **Michael Corbett, The Outsourcing Institute**

That the freeing up of management time was becoming the major issue is made clear in a 1994 study by Investors in Industry that showed this cited by over 80 per cent of a survey sample, just ahead of outsourcing's ability to reduce staff costs. That same survey also illustrated the problems of outsourcing. Quality of the vendor's service was the overwhelming complaint, with communications with the outsourcer second and redundancy costs third.

Take the time to get it right

What must be realized for anyone embracing the outsourcing process is why they are doing it. Being honest with themselves, or the team making honest, collective decisions is paramount. If you are outsourcing to save costs quickly and brutally, admit it. Trying to create a strategy out of a one-off, short-term action is just plain stupid. If, on the other hand, you see outsourcing as a long-term part of your overall business process, then take your time and choose your direction and your vendors carefully. On that, Outsourcing Institute's Michael Corbett has some excellent advice to share. 'Basically, we see six steps to the outsourcing process.

■ Strategic analysis
■ Identifying the best candidates
■ Defining the requirements
■ Selecting the providers
■ Transitioning the operations
■ Managing the relationship

Advises Corbett, 'In terms of strategic analysis, we find that organizations are being most successful when they view outsourcing as fundamentally a tool for organizational change.

Outsourcing

When they focus on their core competencies and what the core competencies of their potential providers are. They have to clarify their organizational goals.' He continues, 'Understanding why it is that your organization is outsourcing, what it is trying to accomplish, is critical and is a critical first step in the process.' Getting the process championed from the top, not just tacitly approved, is also vital. 'Leadership comes from the top executive,' stresses Corbett, 'executive direction for the entire process is required and you must recognize that you are in it for the long haul. This is not a short-term tactical decision. What you are really in is the centre of a fundamental reshaping of the organization.'

Now to choosing candidates that meet your requirements. Corbett says that organizations must ask themselves, 'what are the areas within my organization that are not core ? Where will I get the best return on investment from an outsourcing decision ?'

He notes, 'Return on investment we have found is one of the critical questions that has to be asked.' Corbett further advises that you have to take a microscopic look at the people you might consider. 'A lot of discussion goes into defining the scope of an outsourcing relationship.' In defining the requirements of that relationship, Corbett warns that it 'is very difficult, but absolutely crucial, that you define your requirements in clear, complete and measurable terms. A great deal of extra effort is required to do that effectively, but I can't overstate how important that is in the process.' And he believes it is crucial that potential outsourcers 'don't just describe the results they are looking for, but describe the relationship they are looking for and expect.'

Based on the Outsourcing Institute's own research, Corbett suggests that 'one of the things we have found in sharing requirements that sometimes take people a little by surprise when we first say it is be very open in terms of sharing the current problems you are having and you are trying to solve. Share with them what it's costing you to provide those services today and give the outside organization something to compete against – something to beat.' He goes on, 'You're looking to enter into a long-term relationship and the very first way to do that is by creating a sharing of information. We found this to be crucial.'

When beginning the process of selecting partners,

> **Successful outsourcing organizations do a great deal more than what is called for in the 'letter' of the relationship, they really build partnerships.**

Giving people the ownership of your problems makes them your partner, but remember it isn't just a cheap way of doing business. You want the vendor to succeed as well.

Outsourcing at the core of your business

Corbett's view is that 'cultural fit' is the vital criterion. 'Look for organizations,' he suggests, 'with whom you recognize you have a similar way of approaching problems; a similar set of values; a similar set of criteria in terms of how you manage your business.''Select partners based on their total capabilities, not just price or another single aspect of what they can do. Build upon relationships you already have, use references and reputation as a way to identify the right partner. Finally,' he notes, 'negotiate reasonable price and performance measures. This has to be an ongoing relationship, that is going to work for both of the organizations involved – so it is critical to negotiate a tough, but fair, relationship.'

Making the transition to an outsourced relationship is very much tied to the ability of your business to communicate what's going on to all the stakeholders. 'Communicate early and often,' as Corbett points out, 'and allow time for your relationship to mature. Promote successes and as other things start to work well, promote those successes too and use all the communications tools at your disposal to do it.'

In managing the new outsourced relationship, Corbett has the following advice. 'Put as much time and energy into deciding in advance how you are going to manage this relationship as you put into defining the relationship and creating it to begin with. Create a management structure to fit the new organizational realties. What I mean by that is, recognize that you are going to be asking people within your organization to manage in a very different environment than they're used to. So you need to take the time to put that structure in place and give them the support they need. Fundamentally to maintain a win–win focus.'

Corbett's views are amply supported by those of Michael Horder of Coopers & Lybrand, who warns his clients that savings from outsourcing are not guaranteed. Indeed he tells them that there are plenty of costs they need to consider, like redundancy and staff transfers. All the same, Horder makes it clear that outsourcing – to be effective – must be a board-level decision, pointing out the unlikelihood of people currently doing a job agreeing to vote themselves out of one. But he is certain – as are an increasing number of others – that outsourcing is not a fad, but a new way of looking at the business process. 'Outsourcing,' he says, 'is different, because it takes firms a lot of time and money to

find world-class operators in the services they want to contract out.'

But watch out for the workers

**The imperative to outsource may be there, but you do
need to heed any grumblings at the grass roots of your
operation. No-one understands this better than executives
at troubled General Motors – the
USA's most inefficient car maker. Desperate to cut costs,
which means outsourcing and job losses, it is getting
wrapped up in nasty negotiations with unions that may last
a long time. Outside observers have said that 'outsourcing
will be the 900-pound gorilla' and one that could spell
serious long-term strife.**

**This is a classic example of the problem confronting
much of the manufacturing industry. Faced with the need
to cut costs and become more efficient – it takes GM 3.6
people to assemble a car, compared to 3.1 at Ford and
2.09 at Nissan – they are wedged between a rock and a
very hard place indeed. Outsourcing may solve their problems – but at a price and certainly not as a short-term
option.**

A long-term strategic process

PA's study, *International Strategic Sourcing Survey 1996*,
adds further reasons for the adoption of outsourcing as a
long-term, strategic management process. Says the report,
'The main driver of outsourcing is the need for focused competitiveness. This continuing and seemingly universal
increase in the use and scope of outsourcing would appear
to suggest that there is a significant and well-rounded ratio-
nale behind it – it is not simply another "fashion". This is
borne out by the research, in which three views of outsourcing are substantially endorsed:

- We outsource where others can do it better
- We outsource to focus on our core business
- We outsource to reduce our cost base'

But the PA study brings another element into the 'out-

Outsourcing at the core of your business

sourcing as a strategic tool' debate. Suggesting that to be an effective outsourcer in the long-term you need to examine and know what your core competencies are, they note that as few companies seem to have carried out that exercise, the decision to outsource is forcing them to do just that. PA says, 'While organizations recognise they must focus their own resources on things that give competitive or strategic advantage and/or on the things they do better than anyone else, few of them have developed their thinking much beyond this point. For example, there is rarely a clear organizational focus for determining which activities are "core competencies", or for determining strategic impact.' The study goes on to note that outsourcing is a perfect fit with the trend towards more process-oriented organizational structures. 'There is evidence,' PA says, 'that outsourcing is becoming more complex, partly as a result of the general shift towards process-oriented management and partly a result of the shift away from local approaches towards a global dimension.' Furthermore, the PA study closely paralleled the views of the Outsourcing Institute, saying that in the opinions of the organizations they surveyed, the top success criteria for good outsourcing relationships were:

- Activity well defined
- Roles and responsibilities of all parties clear
- Good relationship with supplier
- High quality of supplier
- Effective client management/monitoring

So there we have it. Outsourcing is proving to be more than many executives thought. At one end it might be classified as a fad, a trend of the month, but that is where the concept is being embraced by cost-cutters as a short-term activity. At the other end it is emerging as a key part of the re-engineered management process of some of the world's leading corporations. It looks like outsourcing is more than here to stay, it is a significant part of how many of us will manage tomorrow if we get our initial homework right and choose the right partners.

Executive summary

- Many organizations are still using short-term outsourcing techniques as knee-jerk, 'we're in trouble' cost-cutting exercises.

- Never outsource what you don't understand. Outsource things you *can* do, but would rather not.

- There are now clearly two levels of outsourcing – tactical (short-term, results-driven) and strategic (long-term, process-driven).

- Outsourcing gives managers time to concentrate on the things they do well.

- As organizations become more process driven, outsourcing is a natural fit with new business structures.

- Outsourcing isn't about cost savings, it's about more effective performance.

- Successful outsourcing leaders do more than what is called for in the structure of a shared relationship.

- You never outsource your secrets. Coca-Cola isn't going to outsource its recipe.

- Define your outsourcing requirements in clear, complete and measurable terms.

- Look for outsourcers with whom you have a cultural fit.

- Put as much time and energy into deciding how to manage as you put into defining and creating the outsourcing process to begin with.

3

More about how to do it – and why

Remember when big was beautiful? Remember when doing everything yourself showed you were a force to be reckoned with? No-one knows exactly when the idea that perhaps there were many areas that could be safely, more productively passed out to others, but it has certainly occurred over the last decade. Of course, manufacturing has always been an outsourcer. You only have to lift the hood and look at the engine of a 1950s car to realize that most of the components stuck on to the engine block weren't made in the factory even then, but produced by outside suppliers. Similarly the clothing industry, the defence industry, shipbuilding and white goods all had their need for external suppliers. More recently, the computer industry provided a classic outsourcer's example.

Possibly what has shaken us up more than anything else have been the twin revolutions of IT and the arrival of the global economy at virtually the same time. Technology has given us unparalleled opportunities to do things in different ways, including sourcing from around the world. Add this to a period of recession that forced us out of our traditional ways and thinking and you have a revolution. Outsourcing is a major part of that revolution and is set to remain so.

So far we have looked at some of the forces impacting organizations, the differentiations that are taking place between tactical and strategic outsourcing are some of the ways to begin to ensure that any process you get into has a

Outsourcing

better than average chance of success. Now, with the help of research from the Outsourcing Institute in New York, we can take some of that a little further, examining in more detail why companies outsource. From there we take a look at some of the issues and options that are giving outsourcing a reputation as a key part of the new management process, as well as taking a close look at a fast-rising area of outsourcing – facilities management.

Building an outsourcing relationship that works, according to the Outsourcing Institute, is most often based on three things:

- Reputation
- References
- Existing relationships

An outsourcing relationship is most often based on reputation, references and existing contacts – think of who you already know before you waste lots of time.

So, as you begin to look around for possible 'partners' in some of your business operations, you don't always have to look very far. They may be people you work with in one way or another already, but you don't know the extent of what they could possibly offer you, there may be a possible supplier or potential outsourcer just down the street. Remember, it doesn't have to be a world away to be world-class. Equally, unsuccessful outsourcing relationships are often based on three very different things:

- Finance, legal and vendor issues dominate the decision process
- Vendors are not pre-qualified based on their total capabilities
- Short-term benefits dominate as the reason for outsourcing

So what are the real reasons that companies are increasingly turning to the outsource option? Well, as already seen, perceived or imagined, or even known, cost savings can have a lot to do with it, as can longer-term plans in an increasing number of instances. Using data made available for this book by the Outsourcing Institute in the USA we have been able to put together the top ten reasons that organizations outsource and what they think the potential benefits are:

in brief

'Dispatching work to outsiders is hardly new, Automatic Data Processing began taking over companies' payroll functions in the 1950s. EDS began handling computer and data management in the 1960s ...' – *Business Week*, April 1996

Strategic
■ Improve company focus
■ Access world-class capabilities
■ Accelerate re-engineering benefits
■ Share risks
■ Free resources for other purposes

Tactical
■ Make capital funds available
■ Cash infusion
■ Reduce and control operating costs
■ Resources not available internally
■ Function difficult to manage or out of control

Use outsourcing as a way to get back to basics and improve your business focus – it can be the clean sheet of white paper that all our organizations need from time to time.

The following is the Outsourcing Institute's report and viewpoint on these issues:

We recently completed a trends report, *Outsourcing Purchasing Dynamics – Expectations and Outcomes*. In this study we discovered that overemphasis on short-term benefits is a clear warning sign of an outsourcing project that will prove unsuccessful. When the strategic reasons for outsourcing are overshadowed by short-term business concerns, companies are often disappointed with the results. Outsourcing is a long-term, strategic management tool. For this reason, we review the ten reasons for outsourcing in reverse order of strategic importance. The first five reasons (as shown above) are tactical, near-term issues and the second five are more strategic, long-term benefits.

Outsourcing

Reason 10: Function difficult to manage or out of control
Outsourcing is certainly one option for addressing these types of problems. It does not, however, mean abdication of management responsibility. Nor does it work well as a knee-jerk reaction by companies in trouble. For example in our 1995 Trends Report, 'better operating controls' rated no higher than 4.9 on a ten-point scale as a reason for outsourcing. Companies that did rate 'better control' as an important reason for outsourcing were more likely to be dissatisfied with the results. Why? The reality is that when a function is viewed as 'difficult to manage' or 'out of control' the organization needs to examine the underlying causes. If, for example, the reason is that the requirements, expectations or needed resources are not clearly understood, then outsourcing won't improve the situation – it may in fact exacerbate it.

Reason 9: Resources not available internally
Companies outsource because they do not have access to the required resources within the company. For example, if an organization is expanding its operations, especially into a new geographical area, outsourcing is a viable and important alternative to building the needed capability from the ground up. Or perhaps a major reorganization has divested the company of the resource; or a subsidiary was spun-off, but a needed functional area, such as logistics or a computer data centre, remained with the parent company. In these types of situations, where the required resources would otherwise need to be built from scratch, outsourcing becomes a viable, attractive alternative. Similarly, rapid growth or expansion of operations is a strong indicator that outsourcing may be right for a company.

Reason 8: Reduce and control operating costs
The single most important tactical reason for outsourcing is to reduce and control operating costs. Access to an outside provider's lower cost structure, which may be the result of a greater economy of scale or some other advantage based on specialization, is clearly and simply one of the most compelling tactical reasons for outsourcing. Additionally, companies that try to do everything themselves may incur vastly higher research, development, marketing and deployment expenses – expenses that have to be passed on to the ultimate consumer. Today's

customers are too sophisticated to accept the costs associated with an organization's attempts to maintain singular control over all its resources.

Reason 7: Cash infusion

Outsourcing often involves the transfer of assets from the customer to the provider. Equipment, facilities, vehicles and licences used in the current operations all have a value and are in fact sold to the vendor. The vendor then uses these assets to provide services back to the client and, frequently, to other clients as well. Depending on the value of the assets involved, this sale may result in a significant cash payment to the customer. There is one subtlety of this transaction which needs to be pointed out. When these assets are sold to the vendor, they are typically sold at book value. The book value can be higher than the market value. In these cases, the difference between the two actually represents a loan from the vendor to the client, which is repaid in the price of the services over the duration of the contract. That is, part of the cash is income from the sale of the assets and part is a loan to be repaid.

Reason 6: Make capital funds available

Outsourcing is a way to reduce the need to invest capital funds in non-core business functions. Instead of acquiring the resources through capital expenditures, they are contracted for on an 'as used' operational expense basis. Outsourcing makes capital funds more available for core areas. It can also improve certain financial measurements of the firm by eliminating the need to show return on equity from capital investment in non-core areas. There is tremendous competition within most organizations for capital funds. Deciding where to invest the funds is probably one of the most important decisions that an organization's senior management is called upon to make. For example, when a firm outsources its vehicle fleet, buildings or computers these areas no longer compete for the company's capital. Often these types of investments have been difficult to justify when put into comparison with areas more directly related to producing product or serving the customer.

Reason 5: Free resources for other purposes

Every organization has limits on the resources available to it. The constant challenge is to ensure that its limited

Outsourcing can be a two-way street. You can outsource your non-core business and insource from others who can't match your capabilities.

resources are expended in the most valuable areas. Outsourcing permits an organization to redirect its resources from non-core activities toward activities which have the greater return in serving the customer. Most often the resources redirected through outsourcing are people. By outsourcing non-core functions, the organization can redirect these people, or at least the staff slots they represent, onto greater value-added activities. People whose energies are currently focused internally can now be focused externally – on the customer.

Reason 4: Share risks

There are tremendous risks associated with the investments an organization makes. When companies outsource they become more flexible, more dynamic and better able to change themselves to meet the changing opportunities. Markets, competition, government regulations, financial conditions and technologies, all change extremely quickly. Keeping up with these changes, especially where every new generation requires a significant investment of resources and money, is very difficult and, still today 'bet-your-company' types of investment are all too common. Outsourcing is a vehicle for sharing these risks across many companies. Outsourcing providers make investments not on behalf of just one company, but on behalf of many. By sharing these investments, the risks borne by any single company are significantly reduced. Outsourcing is, in effect, the management tool for becoming what is referred to as 'the modular company', the 'virtual corporation', or the 'agile competitor'.

Reason 3: Accelerate re-engineering benefits

Outsourcing is often the by-product of another powerful management tool – business process re-engineering (BPR). It allows an organization to immediately realize the anticipated benefits of re-engineering by having an outside organization – one that is already re-engineered to world-class standards – take over the process. BPR is the fundamental rethinking of business processes, with the aim of seeing dramatic improvements in critical measures of performance, such as cost, quality, service, and speed. But how are the benefits of re-engineering to be realized and by when? We have found that outsourcing allows an organization to immediately realize the anticipated benefits of BPR by having an outside organization take over the process, saving a lot of executive time needed to be invested in taking an internal function to world-class standards. More and more frequently we are seeing organizations deciding to outsource the function to someone who can immediately guarantee the improvements offered by re-engineering and assume the risks as well. Outsourcing becomes a way to realize the benefits of BPR today, as opposed to tomorrow.

Reason 2: Access to world-class capabilities

By the very nature of their specialization, outsourcing providers can bring extensive world-wide, world-class capability to meet the needs of their customers. Just as their clients are outsourcing to improve their focus, so these vendors have honed their skills at providing the services in which they specialize. Often these vendor capabilities are the results of extensive investments in technology, methodologies and people – investments made over a considerable period of time. In many cases the vendor's capabilities include specialized industry expertise, gained through working with many clients facing similar challenges. This expertise may be translated into skills, processes or technologies, uniquely capable of meeting the outsourcer's needs. Partnering with a world-class provider offers many advantages:

- Access to new technology, tools and techniques that the organization may not currently possess
- Avoidance of the cost of chasing technology and the training/learning costs associated with each new generation breakthrough
- Better career opportunities for [often stagnant or at risk] personnel, who transition to the outsourcing provider
- Enable the outsourcer's staff to concentrate on building new and improved capabilities, that meet future business requirements, rather than concentrating on managing current operations
- Outsourcing providers typically have more structured methodologies, procedures and documentation – as well as larger, more experienced staff, that can pay-off in fewer operational problems
- Competitive advantage through access to expanded skills
- A better price/value mix on investments

Outsourcing

- The providers' primary business is delivering world-class support: these companies have a track record of proven experience and leadership in the application of their speciality to business processes
- Access to better tools and techniques for estimating the costs of new solutions
- Access to hitherto unavailable industry knowledge, experience and expertise that the provider has gained from other clients and partners
- On-site staff to support the client's needs.

Reason One: Improve company focus

Outsourcing lets the company focus on broader business issues, while having operational details assumed by an outside expert. Outsourcing is an organization-shaping management tool which can lead to a clearer, more effective focus on meeting customers needs. For many companies, the single most compelling reason for outsourcing is that several of the 'how' type issues are siphoning off huge amounts of management time and attention. Too often, the resolution of these issues gets stuck in middle management 'decision grid-lock'. Outsourcing creates financial and opportunity costs that affect the organization's future.

That's the Outsourcing Institute's succinct wrap-up of the present state of the art of outsourcing.

What also should be said, is that it scares people too! As dealt with in more detail in Chapter 5, the human issues do need to be stressed as well and some of these, despite the shake-outs going on all around us, are still hard to take.

At the top there are senior management not prepared to take the plunge. In the middle are 'going nowhere' managers protecting their turf and operating on the principle that 'outsourcing is a brilliant concept and I fully advocate its adoption – but in someone else's division'. Lower down junior managers, administrative and clerical staff are distrustful and uneasy. At blue-collar level they are not happy either.

What we have to remember as we embrace outsourcing as a concept to provide new impetus to our businesses is that we might know that, but we are going to have quite a job to convince everyone else. Consider this. What does your workforce read in the newspapers, hear on the radio and see on the TV each day – companies closing down divisions,

The idea of outsourcing scares people too! Communicate, communicate, communicate. Take them along with you – don't leave them wallowing behind in a sea of uncertainty.

relocating people, selling them off to a new supplier, where employment guarantees aren't always there. And it doesn't matter how true that picture is, they have only got to *think* that it's true and it will take more than a month of Sundays to change their perception.

in brief

'The head of one leading management consultancy noted the arrival of what he termed "the Swiss cheese" organization. It has a solid overall form, but is missing pieces.'
– *Human Resources*, January 1995

So, if we all agree that in its 'purest' form outsourcing is a dynamic process that can rejuvenate and rekindle sagging fortunes, let's make sure we tell our managers and workers that message and its one they not only hear, but believe as well. One whiff of downsizing in all this and transitioning becomes a nightmare.

It's all very well to get fired up about strategy, but check out the human element before you get too far.

Checking out best practices

A three-year research project at Templeton College Oxford, Best Practices in Information Technology Sourcing, by Leslie Willcocks and Mary Lacity, showed up some vary real concerns that potential outsourcers (IT or otherwise) need to heed and take into account in their planning.

Beginning with some background into IT outsourcing's development, Willcocks and Lacity illustrate that it isn't always as easy as it might seem from a distance to make outsourcing projects and processes work.

When Eastman Kodak turned over the bulk of its information technology operations to three outsourcing partners in 1989, it triggered an important change in the way IT operations were carried out. Senior executives of other

Fortune 500 companies followed suit and signed long-term contracts worth hundreds of millions of dollars with IT outsourcing partners, including Continental Airlines, Continental Bank, Enron, First City, General Dynamics, McDonnell-Douglas, and Xerox. In the United Kingdom we have seen similar outsourcing deals in companies like BP Exploration, British Aerospace and British Home Stores, and central government departments like the Inland Revenue and the Department of Social Security. By 1994 some 51 per cent of UK organizations were outsourcing some aspect of their information technology needs. In the public sector this trend was encouraged by the government's compulsory competitive tendering initiatives and privatization policies. In the seven years since the surge of outsourcing interest prompted by Kodak, organizations have had ample time to evaluate whether their sourcing ambitions have been realized, and whether outsourcing helps to deliver on the power of IT that increasingly derives from its integration with business operations.

During this three-year research programme we conducted in-depth case studies of sixty-one IT sourcing decisions in forty US and UK companies. We interviewed 145 business executives, chief information officers, outsourcing consultants, and vendor account managers. This rich research base – which includes both successes and failures – enables a range of principles concerning success in sourcing IT activities to be established. Certain of these, mainly relating to timing and perception and to scale of operations, are matters over which organizations have little control. Others, however, offer key lessons for success in creating and managing sourcing. These can be summarized as follows:

1 *Right sourcing is selective sourcing*
Information technology within organizations spans a variety of activities in terms of business contribution, integration with existing processes, and level of technical maturity. Such diversity demands tailored as well as standard solutions. No one vendor or internal IT department possesses the experience and economies of scale to perform all IT activities most effectively. While some activities, especially stable IT activities with

known requirements, can be easily outsourced through services readily available on the marketplace, outsourcing other IT activities requires much management attention, protection, and nurturing to bring about business success.

2 *Tailored contracts are better than 'strategic partnerships'*

Too often the rhetoric of 'strategic partnership' fails to translate into contractual terms which involve shared risks and rewards. Instead, it often results in poorly negotiated contracts which favour the vendors. Vendor account managers are rewarded for maximizing profits, in some instances by charging excess fees for services extending beyond the contract, or by reducing service levels – which in turn reduces the customers' service levels. In contrast, tailored contracts which fully specify costs and requirements are preferable. Tailored contracts involve buying-in vendor expertise to develop new technology, contracting the management and support for a stable, well-defined IT activities or, if based on a long-term relationship, drawing up specifications which take account of complementary as well as shared goals.

3 *Short-term contracts are better than long-term contracts*

Short-term contracts are more preferable to long-term contracts for several reasons. First, technology and business conditions cannot be predicted for more than three years, thus making contracts increasingly outdated as time progresses. Second, short-term contracts motivate vendor performance because vendors realize customers may switch suppliers when the contract expires. Third, short-term contracts allow companies to recover and learn more quickly from mistakes.

4 *Outsourcing often involves substantial hidden costs which need to be carefully ascertained and avoided*

Unanticipated costs are a major drawback that consistently appeared in the deals we studied. Eleven sources of such costs are identified. Many spring from weaknesses in evaluation practice prior to signing contracts. Others involve weaknesses and oversights in contracting. In many cases organizations find themselves paying for the vendor's learning curve, are locked into old technologies with high switching costs, or incur large discretionary spending outside the contract with the vendor in order to maintain required service levels. Companies need to analyse fully and reduce all potential hidden costs before signing outsourcing contracts.

5 *Internal IT departments should be encouraged to bid against external suppliers*

Many vendors' bids are based on efficient management practices which can be replicated by internal IT managers. Often senior executives exclude internal IT departments from the bid process because they believe, as many told us: 'If my IT managers could do this, they would have done it already.' Yet IT managers are frequently held back from implementing best practices because internal politics resist cost reduction tactics such as consolidating data centres, standardizing software packages, or implementing full-cost chargeback systems. Only after senior managers have given a mandate for improvement are IT managers empowered to overcome resistance. Although a vendor's bid may still prevail, by also considering internal bids the organization can assure itself that this is due to labour specialization or economies of scale that cannot be replicated internally.

6 *Sourcing should be decided jointly by senior executives and IT managers*

Successful sourcing decisions require the complementary perspectives of all the players in the process. Senior management can provide the larger business perspective – such as the need for organization-wide cost cuts – as well as the 'muscle' to enforce such business initiatives. IT managers should provide the necessary technical expertise on such matters as service levels, measures of performance, rates of technical obsolescence, rates of service growth, and price/performance improvements as well as the host of other technical insights needed to develop requests for proposals, to evaluate vendor bids, and to negotiate and manage sound contracts.

The need for senior management to participate in the management of IT underlies all these lessons. Although some senior executives perceive IT as a utility or commodity that can be easily transferred *en bloc* to an IT vendor, this perception is based on the dangerous assumption that IT services are the same or that IT can be 'plugged in and out'. This is dangerous for several reasons. Few information technologies operate in isolation. The power of information technology lies rather in its integration with business operations – again a function requiring senior management direction. Even in instances where IT activities can be managed by external vendors, senior management should participate in the coordination, monitoring, and management of such relationships. Finally, technology of itself is useless unless aligned with valid business objectives – a perspective which requires senior management's direction. All sourcing decisions should begin with the perception of IT as a business enabler, in the shape of either support activities or activities which provide a unique competitive advantage.

A long way to go

Whatever best proactive action could be or should be, in reality most managements are loosening their grip either slowly or with some reluctance. An Andersen Consulting study (see Figure 3.1), while predictably showing that those areas regarded as core functions were outsourced least, also found that non-core functions weren't doing that well either – in the UK at least.

Consulting firm defines outsourcing's models

A leading proponent, world-wide, of the outsourcing movement, and one with a major stake in helping companies come to terms and develop the process is Andersen Consulting. In a recent paper, the head of their UK outsourcing practice, Bill Lattimer, suggested that there were five distinct models for outsourcing.

Model One: **Traditional outsourcing involves the transfer of people and assets to a company, which in return offers a**

Outsourcing

service for a price. The outsourcing of IT data operations is an example.

Model Two: A variant of Model One, involves the customer keeping ownership of the assets whilst still transferring the staff and service responsibility to the supplier.

Model Three: Management contracting involves the buying-in of a management team from a supplier, and giving them management control, while retaining the staff and assets in-house. The Ministry of Defence [in the UK], for example, has a management contract for the operation of the Devonport Dockyard.

Model Four: Bureau service involves outsourcing the activity to a centre which also performs the function for many other companies. This would normally not involve the transfer of any staff or assets. An example would be payroll processing.

Model Five: Various types of joint venture are possible in any of the scenarios that which involve the transfer of staff or assets. It is common in Scandinavia, for example, for outsourcers and customers to set up jointly owned companies into which the staff and assets are transferred – and to share the profits. The same results can also be achieved by setting up benefit-sharing arrangements under any of the other models.

But while many managers might still consider outsourcing as something that manufacturing companies do with parts and components, the fastest-moving areas have been in business services. True business service providers, notably in IT and HR systems, have been making major inroads into manufacturing as well, but it is the service organizations themselves that have seen much of the action as far as outsourcing is concerned. And with a Western world more and more geared to services, this sector not only requires some attention, but in particular can provide pointers that all of us – manufacturer, retailer or service provider – can learn from.

One area that is perhaps just beginning to rate some interest is the global purchasing – or outsourcing – of services. Currently, global purchasing of commodities is quite common, but getting services into line around the world has proven a much more difficult task, due to the often local nature of a myriad suppliers and outworkers.

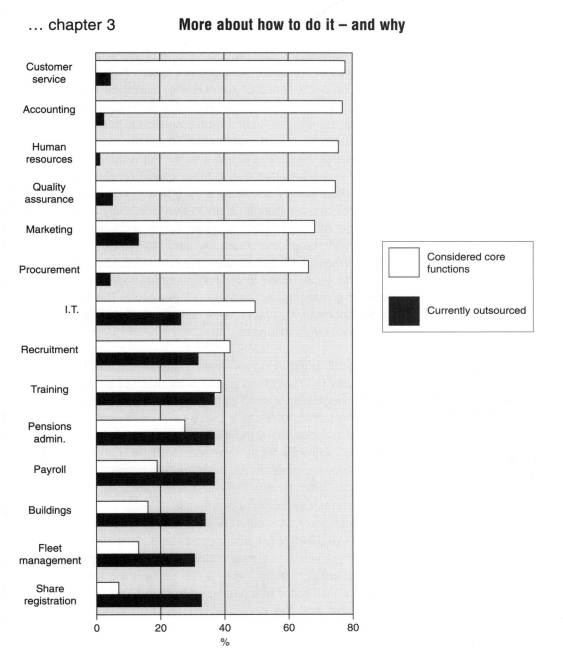

Figure 3.1 Outsourcing may be gaining ground in non-core business areas but it still has a long way to go to get majority acceptance. Areas like recruitment, payroll, pension, training and building management lead but still represent a penetration of less than a third of UK organizations. *Source*: *Outsourcing – Seizing the Strategic Initiative*: Andersen Consulting 1994

Outsourcing

To examine the problem, ISS – one of the world's leading providers of facilities management systems and processes – carried out a series of surveys and workshop discussions during 1995 to determine what the future held for this sort of service. Simply put, was a global service to business really what companies were looking for? To put the whole research programme into context, ISS carried out a survey with 140 senior executives that showed that 'global purchasing is currently more widely practised with regard to commodities (35 per cent of respondents) than to services. Only a small per centage of respondents claimed to have global contracts already in place for professional services (19 per cent), covering areas like legal, accounting and advertising services, with the figure even lower for industrial services, such as cleaning catering and security (15 per cent). The figures for pan-European contracts were similar. ISS's findings were summarized as follows:

World-class business service providers are beginning to offer regional and global solutions as opposed to local or national. If you're in that league, it may be the way to go – very soon.

■ Global purchasing of commodities is currently more widely practised than global purchasing of services.

■ Although only a small percentage of respondents already have global contracts in place for professional and industrial services, many more see the benefits of such services.

■ The petrochemical, transport/vehicle manufacturing, telecommunication and electronic industries are moving faster than others to reap the benefits of global/pan-European servicing agreements.

■ There are major differences in the knowledge and skill-sets required to purchase goods as distinct from services. Companies must equip their purchasing organizations with the right skills if they are to achieve the real benefits of cross-border purchasing agreements.

■ Almost half the organizations involved in the research expressed interest in the global/pan-European purchase of industrial services, such as catering, cleaning and building maintenance, with the same per centage expressing interest in purchasing professional services in this way too.

■ The cost savings available by grouping contracts at a global/pan-European level are not achieved by reducing process or margins, but by working closely with suppliers to improve productivity, reduce the costs of delivery and transfer best-practice across sites.

More about how to do it – and why

■ Global/pan-European service purchasing agreements are considered to have a major role in helping companies to outperform the competition.

■ The success of such agreements will depend largely on the ability of customer and supplier to win the support of those managers in their respective organizations who will be responsible for implementing and further developing the relationship. Only thus can internal resistance be avoided.

■ Geographical presence in several countries is not considered sufficient to qualify a supplier as a global/pan-European partner. Suppliers must also have the culture, structure, systems and people in place to manage cross-border accounts.

■ The way forward begins with clear top management vision and commitment, supplier identification against a commonly agreed set of selection criteria and a viable system for monitoring and measuring supplier performance against mutually agreed targets.

With ISS estimating that in the USA alone a 'staggering $250 billion is spent each year on maintenance, repairs and operating supplies (MRO), that include items as varied as staplers, mops and spare parts', it is no surprise they are trying to get the world's multinational operators interested. One source they quote – that ISS coyly fails to identify – estimates that 'high volume purchasing can trim bills for services and MRO by 10-25 per cent. By comparison, establishing nationwide contracts for raw materials or components now saves only two to five per cent. As the compass narrows in materials, companies are discovering in services and MRO a lost, lush continent for cost reduction.'

ISS – and others like Johnson Controls – know that as outsourcing gains momentum and gets more and more global, their chances of grazing (perhaps the term should be gorging) on that so-called lost, lush continent are getting better and better by the day. Not surprising. To many, keen to divest non-core activities, this will make good dollars and sense as they used to say. ISS comments on the coming windfall: 'Because service purchasing has, to some extent, been neglected, we believe that organizations with large budgets for cleaning and other non-core, labour intensive services are missing opportunities to reap considerable

Outsourcing

benefits, not just in terms of reducing costs, but also in terms of improving service quality. One major European conglomerate we are working with has calculated that cleaning accounts for 10 per cent of its annual $1.5 billion 'occupancy' costs. Add to this the administrative expenses of dealing with an estimated 1000 suppliers, and the incentive to find more streamlined and efficient purchasing processes is obvious.' ISS continue, 'We are already helping organizations with large budgets for low-skilled, labour-intensive services to reduce their costs by 10 to 15 per cent at a national level. By entering into long-term [outsourcing] relationships, where the focus is on specifying the results of the service (the 'outputs'), rather than the manning and frequencies (the 'inputs'), we can maximize our customers' return on spend by dramatically improving productivity. If this can be done globally, the results could be spectacular.' Waldemar Schmidt, ISS's European managing director, sums up the opportunity: 'The challenge for both suppliers and purchasers is to work together to reconcile corporate and local purchasing manager's interests. If this can be achieved, the resulting cost-savings will go straight to the bottom-line.'

One of the key findings that ISS found in their research was that 'building the knowledge, skills and systems required to develop greater capabilities in service purchasing departments seems to be one of the major issues which organizations interested in global service agreements need to address.'

Three companies went on the record with their views in the ISS report:

Remember the purchasing department? Suddenly it's important. But do they know enough to meet today's mixed bag of outsourcing requirements?

1 The general manager of Kodak Facilities Management said: 'The purchase of services is very complicated. In short, a lot of things can go wrong: you can't apply commodity purchasing criteria to a service supply contract. You need to set up systems for monitoring performance and procedures for improving quality; it's not simply a case of reviewing the contract after three years, it's a day-to-day relationship between the customer and the supplier. You can't just walk away and let the thing run itself.'

2 The manager of purchasing and travel operations of Rank Xerox said: 'You have to recognize that professional purchasing grew up in a manufacturing environment. In a

manufacturing environment, buying piece parts or semi-
conductor components or raw materials, i.e. something
that goes into something you sell as a company, is a very
different process. It is controlled, it has specifications. You
can do value engineering, you have all these tools. But,
historically, purchasing does not have a strong footprint in
the non-production area.'

3 An executive of Mobil Europe Purchasing said: 'You know
where you are with a product, but service provision is ultimately dependent on people and there's the problem. A
service supplier may have an international capability, but
you are always reliant on the quality of the local office.
Performance may vary considerably from country to
country.'

There may be doubters like the three above, but ISS and
others see that the rise and rise of global – or at least pan-
European and other regional – service agreements are going
to be inevitable. The main reason will possibly, as with other
decisions to take more and more down the outsourcing
route, be based initially on cost. If a competitor is making
major savings – like those forecast here – and is passing
them on to the customer, the employees or the investors,
they are going to have to play the same game.

ISS, with annual revenues heading toward the $2 billion
mark and with 125 000 employees, is the world's largest
cleaning and facilities service group. Operating in thirty-four
countries in Europe, North America, Latin America and Asia,
they are in a position to push this debate further (Figure 3.2).

Here's how ISS regard the debate so far, adding a veiled
threat to those who do not pay attention to what the future
might hold. 'Purchasing, for many years considered a function which could add little value to business performance, is
currently undergoing a revolution. As the benefits of high-
volume, cross-border purchasing agreements become more
apparent, businesses are seizing opportunities, not only to
reduce significantly their purchasing bills, but also to harness
the creativity and resources of their suppliers in their bid to
outperform the competition. Those organizations which do
not explore these opportunities run the risk of being severely
disadvantaged in the future.' This is how ISS view their
future. 'From the point of view of service providers, a whole
new horizon is opening, which offers considerable rewards to

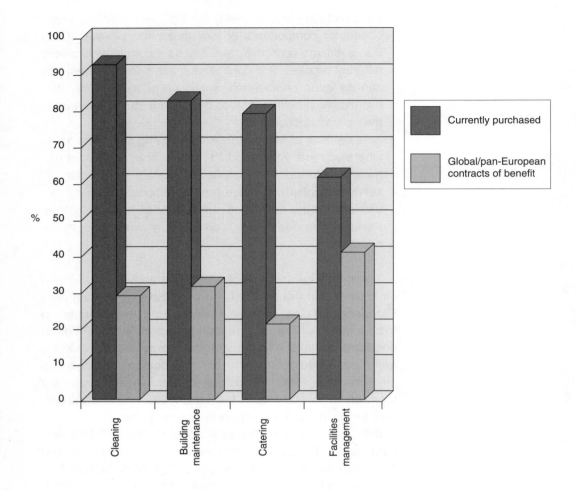

Figure 3.2 The global activities of ISS. (*Source*: *Trends in Global/pan-European Service Purchasing*, ISS, 1995)

those who can rise to the challenge. Like their customers, they must address complex and far-reaching issues. Merely operating in several countries will not be sufficient. Offering a genuine global/pan-European service will involve recruiting, training and retaining highly competent business managers with the ability and skills to develop and expand cross-border opportunities. An organizational structure which is globally cohesive, yet responsive to local needs will be another key determinant for success. Management information systems will need to be tuned to provide the level and type of detail which the customer requires to manage his purchasi processes competitively. And this is just the beginning.'

More about how to do it – and why

Stories about the demise of the one-man window-cleaning business can now be told. But seriously, ISS and its competitors pose a huge threat to national-based operations working with international companies. With the type of savings they claim, eventually multinationals will give it a try. Like other outsourcing initiatives, the imagination that something can be achieved and the will to make it happen is more than half the battle.

The rise and rise of facilities management

Facilities management (FM) – of which ISS is a major global player – has not only come of age, it is overshadowing a lot of other outsourcing areas as well. Now clearly recognized – even by managers in other disciplines – as a business area in its own right, much of that has come about by the bundling-up of the myriad bits and pieces of what was often perceived as the bottom end of business. Rarely has anyone ever waxed lyrical about office cleaning or catering service, building or grounds maintenance. By tying all these areas together and giving them a new, respectable label, FM is not only becoming respectable, it's making money.

External FM outsourcing is really doing excellently what companies have done poorly – or ignored completely – themselves. There's nothing clever about it, just a new focus on something you dismissed as unimportant.

One of the biggest drivers in the rise of FM – sometimes referred to as Business Support Services – has once again been cost coupled to the realization that if anything wasn't core to the business, it was these profit draining rather than profit-making areas that no-one wanted to manage anyway. Until organizations began to specialize in these areas no-one had ever thought of making a career out of them – let alone telling anyone it was part of their responsibilities. Having building maintenance as part of your job description was the corporate equivalent of being sent to the gulag.

All the same, early attempts to outsource these non-productive peripherals were by no means always successful. Enthusiastic amateurs were often the best-fitting description. Equally, it wasn't always the case that a company's purchasing department – probably solely concerned with buying components – could embrace these new needs of top management. As *Human Resources* magazine noted, 'Outsourcing smacked of the cheap and cheerful … like factoring, it somehow didn't 'feel' right'.

Then, almost overnight, something changed, as *Human Resources* explained. 'Partly this was through the growing professionalism of well-managed professional firms like Group 4, Hoskyns and Gardner Merchant.' They noted that suddenly outsourced services were better, more efficient, cost effective and 'best of all, perhaps, the responsibility for managing all this lay outside the company. Not only was outsourcing cheaper, but the problems associated with absence, sickness, regulatory compliance, training and so on landed on someone else's desk.'

in brief

'Outsourcing has become integral to business life. Companies have started acting on the concept of the shamrock organization, created by Charles Handy ..., dividing themselves into a small professional core of employees, a group of flexible, part-time workers and a set of contracted-out or outsourced activities.' – *Outsourcing – Seizing the Strategic Initiative*, **Andersen Consulting, 1994**

What FM has done is turn traditional ways of managing all these non-core areas on its head. Says Gail Hartley of Mowlem Facilities Management, a major UK-based provider, 'traditionally, organizations have not managed their facilities and working environment as an integrated operation. Today, facilities services are increasingly being managed as a discrete function, rather than by a number of separate departments. Organizations,' she says, 'have begun to focus on and realize the strategic contribution their facilities management can bring to the company.' Gail Hartley's explanation of FM is as follows. 'As a relatively new discipline, FM focuses business attention on how support services can contribute to the achievement of the organization's goals. This helps to underline the diverse needs for control and responsibility and to obtain value, quality and efficiency. Ideally, this is accommodated through a single facilities management provider with a single point of contact.' She adds, 'There have been many attempts to define facilities management, but a useful guide is that the "most effective facilities management functions incorporate the management of accommodation, business and staff support services to meet business needs".'

According to Hartley, in the Mowlem facilities management model, there are four distinct areas of FM:

■ Real estate management
■ Premises occupation management
■ Business support management
■ Staff support management

Under these broad headings, Mowlem covers most of any organization's non-core, non-productive, cost-incurring business activity. They provide a useful checklist for initiating an FM outsourcing programme:

■ *Real estate management*: management of the land and property portfolio, leases, insurance, new investment
■ *Premises occupation management*: maintenance, energy management, cleaning, water, sewage, interior and exterior landscaping, fitting out and alterations, health and safety, relocation
■ *Business support management*: security, storage, stationery, printing and reprographics, communications, post room, reception, furniture, fleet vehicles, IT, disaster recovery
■ *Staff support management*: catering, sports, social and welfare facilities.

However, within the FM industry there seem to be distinct differences about what FM actually covers. As Iain Kent of the Centre for Facilities Management at Strathclyde Graduate Business School in Scotland points out, 'In times of economic recession, non-core activities become the focus for cost-saving exercises. As a result, outsourcing of non-core activities to third parties has become a popular trend with many organizations, both from the public and the private sector.' He continues, 'The activities which have tended to be contracted out have been grouped together under the heading of facilities management, by suppliers and buyers

Outsourcing

alike. The result is that it is difficult to discern exactly what activities are being considered under the FM heading.'

Kent concludes that there are a total of six key categories (infrastructure management, transport and telecommunications, environmental management, building operations and maintenance, information technology, support services), but also suggests that 'as yet, there seems little evidence of comprehensive facilities management services being offered over the range of facilities and across the sectorial boundaries of these six categories. Suppliers who do offer a range of services,' Kent believes, 'tend to do so within the confines of one or two of the areas.' He then adds the disquieting observation that 'there is also evidence that suppliers are moving into application areas where their expertise is limited because of demands being placed on them by clients. This obviously will have implications for the quality of services provided, where much of the supply is on a first-time basis.'

Potential outsourcers of FM services should heed Kent's advice and make certain that they take all the precautions they can to ensure that any service provider knows what he or she is doing.

Outsourcing facilities management – a provider's view

Facility management provider Procord – a division of Johnson Controls – is one of the world's leaders in taking over the management of much of the back-room and basic areas of an organization's needs. In an interview, Kevan Wooden, Procord's European Controller, reflects on the growing importance and practicality of outsourcing facilities management (FM).

■ *What areas does facilities management typically cover?* **As far as Procord is concerned, our business is relatively biased towards property management and business support services. However, examples of outsourcing can reach far wider than this. There is usually nothing sacred, only what the client perceives as non-core; and this perception varies client by client.**

More about how to do it – and why

Services like catering are often outsourced, while companies often consider financial services is a good deal more sensitive.

■ *You talk of Procord's FM services as a 'one-stop shop'. What exactly does that cover?* Maintenance, cleaning, security, reprographics, catering, stationery, mailroom, helpdesks, engineering, occupational health, transport and logistics, building management systems, property management of tenants, procurement, stores, contract management. In addition our consulting services cover benchmarking, FM re-engineering, workplace solutions, real estate strategy, health and safety/CDM planning, space planning, outsourcing, contract specification.

■ *What for you are the main reasons companies are outsourcing?* Well, apart from the market testing programme that is being pushed by the present government, I think that there are three main drivers:

Driver One: Because there are cost reductions achievable through using an expert: procuring services with greater concentrated purchasing leverage; re-engineering process and innovating 'best-of-breed' solutions available to the expert by cross-learning on other accounts; people productivity.

Driver Two: The opportunity to make breakthrough change. That is, taking the opportunity of working with an external source to start again with a fresh sheet of paper, thus breaking down overnight all the internal malpractices that would otherwise take an age to demolish.

Driver Three: Finding a better solution for employees. Although this is not always immediately obvious, you find that facilities engineers, for example, can become more motivated by suddenly being part of a company's front line and core business as opposed to being the back-room 'hot potato' in a large corporate environment.

■ *What do you see as the winners and losers in FM outsourcing and why?* The leaders in the private sector have been the large corporates who tend to get recognition as innovators; in particular I would say pharmaceuticals, oil and IT. The followers are retail (perhaps because their diverse geographical outlets are not conducive to economies of scale gained by FM), education

Outsourcing

(the decision-making process is local and thus does not get captured by national marketing), heavy industry (primarily because the culture does not tend to be very innovative).

■ *What would you say are the main barriers to FM outsourcing gaining a foothold in an organization?* Three come immediately to mind: lack of management buy-in; inability to feel comfortable delegating the task; bad prior experience. The key is for the organization to have the right management skills to cope with a devolved relationship. That means a partnership, reporting by exception and occasional audit, rather than hands-on contractual management, requiring client instruction for each task. The better FM companies will run both client and supplier monthly measurement systems, to ensure customer satisfaction and innovate programmes to keep the business moving forward.

■ *How do you ensure that the services you provide as an outsourcer meet the needs of your customer?* Both Procord and Johnson Controls operate a supplier evaluation programme. This involves a team evaluating all the aspects of a supplier, for example management, communication, policy/outline, people, product, training, project management and operating controls. However, I believe that true partnerships will be created from something wider. This will be when the outsourcer and the subcontractors:

- share goals
- share systems and processes
- share investment and innovation
- share risk and rewards.

Seven steps to successful facilities management

A study sponsored by Mowlem Facilities Management and published by The Business Round Table can help ease worries and takes the FM story further, suggesting 'seven steps to successful FM'. The seven steps provide a useful managers guide to the option of FM outsourcing:

Step one: Appoint a client representative

From day one, it is important to identify the right person

More about how to do it – and why

within your organization to act as an 'intelligent client'. A single point of contact, who understands your business – not just its operation, but also its values and long-term goals – is essential to coordinate views within the organization and, if necessary, interpret the market for external service providers. There may already be a facilities management team responsible for identifying areas of need and opportunities for change. If not, an individual – or team – should be appointed to oversee the FM review. The 'client representative' should demonstrate a sound knowledge of existing arrangements and should command strong organization support. He or she should occupy a senior executive position, with a voice at top management level.

Step two: Review existing services

Before planning future FM services, the facilities manager will map out the existing regime to evaluate services in the context of company culture. For example, what criteria are used by the organization to source goods and how does the provision of FM services compare? How is the balance between quality and price determined and should this be re-examined? Priority should be given to services of high value and complexity or those which carry a high core business risk. In some cases it may be useful to commission an independent review by a third party.

Step three: Specifying

An assessment of current FM provision will identify user demand and the need for services. Specification will formalize those conclusions. Understanding how people work is a prerequisite for setting levels of performance. Specification often requires the facilities manager to translate service into technical or performance standards, against which in-house or external providers will be judged. This process may result in a contract between users and the service provider, specifying what it is that users need and how and when it should be delivered.

Step four: Option appraisal

Once the kind of FM service required has been identified, the organization must decide whether to do it in-house or seek an external provider. For those organizations already engaged in an FM programme, the option appraisal may result in an in-house service being contracted out, or an externalized FM service being brought back within the company. Option appraisal will also consider the type of

Outsourcing

service: should there be a single service contract, or a package deal drawing together several services? Should the organization go for a total FM service, relinquishing hands-on management or should it opt for a management agency which will deal directly with the individual companies?

Step five: Selecting your FM supplier

It may be advantageous for the organization to re-tend externally on a regular basis – to play the market. On the other hand, the FM client may be looking for a long-term partnering arrangement [see later] with a chosen supplier in order to secure cost-effectiveness and stability. The organization should have a clear view of how it would conduct the selection process and how it will test competitive bids for quality. FM clients can obtain a clear understanding of the supplier market by calling up material published by suppliers, visiting exhibitions, networking with other facilities managers and vetting FM providers for inclusion on a preferred suppliers register.

Step six: Managing the relationship

Negotiations are necessary to integrate the resources of supplier and client. Outsourcing FM may involve the transfer of staff to an external provider for the first time, or a transfer from one supplier to another. It is important to establish the right relationship from the start. While tender documentation may be fine-tuned into an effective working manual, defining the service itself – and the risk/reward relationship – client and supplier must invest time understanding the working culture, establishing lines of contact, providing for conflict management and above all, making sure that the people interacting are briefed, confident and motivated.

Step seven: Developing the service

Facilities management is a continuous process: change improvement, strategic planning, auditing. It is important to get user feedback on requirements and performance. Benchmark what you do against the competition and always be aware of what the market is offering. Never forget that you might be able to secure better results from your present supplier, or a better deal from elsewhere.

Choosing an FM service

Deciding what's right for your organization is not always easy. The Mowlem Facilities Management-sponsored report, *Thinking About Facilities Management*, provides some useful pointers that examine the advantages and disadvantages of three types of service:

Be careful what you buy, how you buy it and who you buy it from – quick decisions don't pay off!

■ Managing agent
■ Managing contractor
■ Total facilities management

Option One: Managing agent
A contract exists between the customer and the managing agent organization which manages service contracts. Specific works or service contracts are between the customer and the various contractors. The managing agent may manage the customer's own staff and fulfil the role of client representative. Possible advantages are:

■ A modular contract structure offers maximum flexibility – individual contracts may be altered without the need to alter others.
■ Competition on a value-for-money basis is maximized with open competition both for the management role and the works or service subcontracts.
■ If the employer is dissatisfied with the performance of the managing agent, the contract may be renegotiated without the need to nullify, assign or otherwise jeopardize the various contracts between the customer and the works or service providers.

Possible disadvantages are:

■ Gaps may exist between the provision of different packages – technical specifications must try to avoid letting this happen.
■ Although the managing agent will carry out most of the contract letting and administration, there is usually more paperwork with separate contracts and separate monthly payments.

Outsourcing

Option two: Managing contractor
A contract exists between the customer and the managing contractor. Sub-contractors have a direct contractual link with the managing contractor, *not* the customer. Possible advantages are:

- A single point of contact for the customer, transferring administration and payment to the managing contractor, without reducing the control the customer has over individual payments to sub-contractors.
- The level of accountability is very clear – under a single contract relationship, the managing contractor must ensure there are no gaps in service provision.
- Opportunities for competition may be fewer than with the management agent option, but open-book tendering may be used for [transparency of] support services.

Possible disadvantages are:

- Flexibility may be reduced unless provision is built into the contract for variations, as it will be more difficult to add services or terminate the agreement without significant disruption.
- If a third-party agreement is needed (e.g. a collateral warranty for design work, where the sub-contractor must be directly responsible to the customer) the customer must take over the liability and responsibilities of the managing contractor.
- A higher level of auditing is required as budgetary responsibility is devolved.

Option three: Total facilities management (TFM)
The TFM organization supplies – for a fixed price – *all* support services through directly employed staff or by using outside suppliers. Instead of works or service contracts being provided in separate packages by individual companies, the customer puts out tenders only for the primary contract. Possible advantages are:

- A single point of contact for the customer
- The TFM contractor must ensure no gaps exist between specifications

More about how to do it – and why

■ A single contract to management reducing administration to a minimum

Possible disadvantages are:

■ Value-for-money opportunities are reduced as competitive tendering for which the customer receives benefit is only provided once (the TFM organization will keep discounts or benefits from sub-contractors).
■ Less control over sub-contractors
■ Inflexibility makes it difficult to change works or service specifications or add/omit properties to or from the contract
■ If the TFM contract is terminated so are the various service organizations

Take care before tuning into FM

In the coming years, the FM market is going to get tougher, with more competitors and more choice. Make sure you can take advantage of those changes – don't get locked into long-term, inflexible agreements.

Frankly, there seems to be a lot of euphoria around that outsourcing non-core activities is the way to go. But take care! Certainly there are many well-respected FM organizations with solid track records that it would be a pleasure to do business with. Conversely, there are a lot of others who are climbing on a bandwagon replete with rich pickings.

A report by Pye Tait Associates for the UK's Department of Trade and Industry, while noting that 'the major companies are world-size with some being clearly world-class', hands out the following warnings and concerns: 'The lack of a clear and commonly understood definition hinders sectoral awareness and sector-directed activities. The existence of multiple trade associations aggravates the lack of self-awareness and hinders internal development. The second lacks an identity and this hampers the current development as well as future marketing.' The report goes on, 'While human resources are its main asset, the sector remains weak in training across all levels and types of employee,' while it adds, 'heavy reliance on part-time and temporary labour make it difficult to train and maintain standards.' All the same, the Pye Tait report estimates that the FM sector in the U.K. is valued at over £10 billion annually and employs almost 700 000 people. But they also point out that one of the reasons for the growth of this market is that entry costs – partly due to the impermanent nature of the jobs that are

Outsourcing

being done – are very low, with potentially high gains.

That point is stressed by Iain Kent of the Strathclyde Graduate Business School. He points out that 'The FM industry is characterized by intense competition and a lack of commonality between suppliers of FM services, both in terms of their service offering and approach to the market.' Kent goes on, 'Research indicates that barriers to entry to this market are considered to be low and general market opinion is that the number of entrants will continue to grow. Facilities management is a buzzword at the moment,' he says, 'and everyone seems to want a piece of the action.' He predicts that 'As the market settles down, the potential client base for FM will become better educated and clearer in terms of their service requirements. Educated clients will provide higher barriers to entry as suppliers have to meet stricter and more clearly defined criteria.'

So, whatever your outsourcing requirements might be – and especially those in FM, where you might think you can really save a great amount of money with one quickly negotiated contract – take heed. Follow some of these checklists, get a trusted executive to set it up and manage it and never lose sight of other options.

A quick facilities management checklist

A Business Round Table research project entitled *Thinking About Facilities Management* and sponsored by Mowlem – a leading UK FM provider – gives a quick checklist to the things you should keep in mind when considering outsourcing FM services.

Initial selection checklist
- Clients – how many does the supplier have, what industries are they in?
- Track record – what is the supplier's financial status and management capability? What experience does to supplier have in your industry sector? What is their current workload?
- Insurance – will it cover the scope of work required?
- Company culture – what is the supplier's style of deliv-

ery and management and how does it fit in with your organization?
- **Coverage** – can the supplier demonstrate detailed local knowledge, but also offer the same service between sites?
- **Relationships** – how well are the supplier's staff, existing clients and sub-contractors handled?
- **Resources** – what staff skills, equipment and technology are at the supplier's disposal? Is there the [long-term] technical and management expertise to meet your requirements?
- **Risk** – is the supplier clear about the risks and responsibilities and willing to accept them?
- **Unique selling points (USPs)** – what differentiates the supplier from their competitors?
- **Policy** – does the supplier have policies on health, safety, quality, recruitment, training, the environment?
- **Support** – does the supplier have systems such as helpdesks, planned preventative maintenance systems, booking systems to support clients on-site?

... and one of my own. Don't forget that gut feel counts for just as much – possibly more – than all the proposals, platitudes and promises!

Outsourcing can and will play a critical role, especially in these non-core business areas, but don't go out and build problems that you then have to spend a great deal of management time unravelling. The saying is that there is no point in buying a dog and then barking yourself. Unless managed properly and professionally from the outset, outsourcing can force you to do just that.

Executive summary

- **An outsourcing relationship is most often based on reputation, references and existing contacts.**

- **Use outsourcing as a way to get back to basics and improve your business focus.**

Outsourcing

- When outsourcing is linked solely to short-term concerns, companies are often disappointed with the results.
- Don't forget that the idea of outsourcing scares people too! Take them along with you – don't leave them wallowing behind.

- There has been a rush to outsource business services and it's still going on.

- World-class business service providers are beginning to offer regional and global solutions as opposed to local or national.

- Suddenly, the purchasing department's important. But do they know enough to meet today's outsourcing requirements?

- External FM outsourcing is really doing excellently what companies have done poorly – or ignored completely – themselves.

- Be careful what you buy, how you buy it and who you buy it from.

- The FM market is going to get tougher and offer more choice. Make sure you can take advantage.

4

A suitable case for outsourcing

There comes a time when it becomes necessary to show just what outsourcing is capable of and what companies are trying to achieve. In this chapter there are two distinct types of examples. First, you will see that in the following pages there are a series of mini-cases (most of these based on news stories and our own desk research) that serve to show the extent and types of outsourcing that are currently being implemented or considered. The intention is to give a broad view of outsourcing's capabilities and possibilities. Within the examples there are certain to be ideas and options that you and your organization can adopt or adapt. Indeed, I would think that this is the largest selection of outsourcing examples ever assembled. Second, there are a series of more detailed cases of how individual organizations are either focusing on their core competencies by using outsourcing as a strategic weapon or businesses that have evolved to take advantage of other corporations' needs to divest parts of their operation.

in brief

'Many times the needed expertise is in fact "under foot" – it just requires the proper guidance and management.' **Robert Vrancken**

They outsourced an island!

This might be a little wacky, but it shows what imagination can do. Johnson Controls have outsourced a complete island for the US Army. Kwajalein Island was a US Army missile testing base and the firm provided every municipal service including policemen, firefighters, lifeguards, teachers, trash-collectors, waiters and so on.

Doing it with DHL

When you are considering outsourcing and what your business really means – and what those core competencies are – consider what this organization has done.

Along with its competitors in the packing a shipping business, DHL long ago realized that smart organizations don't want to deliver themselves, don't want to worry about the logistics and don't want to hold on to costly inventory. Now known as integrators, DHL, Fedex, UPS and others are helping cash-strapped companies eliminate warehouses and delivery networks, packing goods for them and ensuring on-time delivery.

That's outsourcing at one end of the spectrum for DHL. But at the other end, the company itself is passing out work. Aware that the last thing it required was thousands of vans and trucks that needed maintaining and paying for, it has embarked on a programme of outsourcing its street-by-street delivery. Beginning in countries like the U.K. and Italy, where more open legislation makes it easy to start, they have outsourced much of their customer delivery service to owner/drivers. Sure, they supply the uniform, have the driver's truck sprayed in the DHL colours (even help the driver get a loan to buy the truck in some instances), but it's not their truck.

Some drivers now operate more than one truck, hiring their own people. Apart from saving on inventory and tying up assets, are there any other advantages? You bet! DHL report productivity gains of up to 40 per cent as owner/drivers get paid per piece they pick up and deliver. Oh, and something else. Since the receptionist is often the 'buyer' of the service, it is in the owner/driver's interest to smile and give better than usual customer satisfaction – so that's up too.

Hooker Cockram builds an outsourcing reputation

Hooker Cockram is a 130-year-old construction company, headquartered in the State of Victoria in Australia. One of the biggest local companies in Victoria, they decided in 1988, under the guidance of their chairman Peter Clark, to change entirely the way they worked – moving from a traditional construction organization to a group that would keep its core competencies as a finder and supervisor of building projects, but began to outsource everything they did not regard as crucial core operations – from as wide a spectrum as possible that included design staff on one side and construction crews on the other.

According to their present managing director Bob Milne, Hooker Cockram set up its long-term plan based on three basic tenets of how it would operate:

- Our vision
- Our business
- Our mission

Says Milne, 'our vision is to be the best Australian commercial/industrial construction company, with a reputation for excellence, integrity and trust. Our business is the provision of a broad range of management skills that facilitate the construction of new buildings and the refurbishing of existing premises for our clients. These skills complement our strengths as a traditional builder and are available at all stages of a project from inception to commissioning.' Milne points out that their mission as an organization has six distinct parts:

1 'To ensure successful project outcomes for our clients by applying our people resources, experience, innovative approach and building skills

Outsourcing

2 To create an exciting working environment that stimulates our people, consultants and contractors to achieve their full potential

3 To continuously improve our systems, technology and project delivery to achieve excellent performance in all areas of our operations

4 To help our stakeholders embrace the challenges of a rapidly changing work environment with enthusiasm and confidence

5 To meet consistently high performance standards on our projects in terms of time, quality and cost

6 To steadily increase the value of our shareholders' equity.'

The firm, with clients like BP, Glaxo, Merck, McDonald's, Esso, Mars and Upjohn, made a decision that flew in the face of traditional construction groups. What they would do was go back to the drawing board and recreate their company in a way that would allow them to better manage projects for their clients, by holding on to what they did best and out-sourcing the very best skills they could get from other vendors, to provide a complete design to delivery package.

They decided to build working relationships that were interlocking and synergistic based on a long-term versus a short-term basis. To indicate the variety of ways they viewed these relationships and who would be involved, they list seven different relationship categories:

- Friends
- Partners (psychological and emotional)
- Legal partners
- Joint ventures
- Vendor agreements
- Strategic alliances with customers
- Strategic alliances with partners

Additionally, their view was that building relationships for the long term had to involve a transfer of knowledge and a steady build-up of trust and understanding of how each other worked.

What Hooker Cockram did was to build their organization and the relationship with their outside partners, clients and suppliers on the ongoing improvement and development of the following precepts:

A suitable case for outsourcing

- Enhancing and sharing knowledge
- Interpersonal skills
- Negotiation skills
- Team effectiveness
- Lifestyle skills
- Partnering
- Networking
- Mentoring and coaching
- Technical skills

Their plan was to change both their organization and those they worked with by leading them down the same path that would change the way all of them worked and how they thought about the business and the client. To do this they focused on five key areas that would create the sought-after interdependency:

- Increase integration
- Managing new control forms
- Giving up old behaviours
- Focus on partnering
- Trust as an essential

In creating the network Hooker Cockram kept what it considered its core business areas in-house. These were:

- Project management
- Construction management
- Cost planning
- Design management
- Financial management
- Project accounting
- Scheduling
- Quality management
- Procurement
- Client reporting
- Team building

At the same time they outsourced:

- Master planning
- Architectural design
- Engineering design

Outsourcing

- Process design
- Validation
- Training
- Equipment supply/vendors
- Trade contractors

In this way they have gone from an organization that tried to do everything itself in-house in 1986 to a networked, out-sourced organization that boasts an external support system that includes architects, engineers and process designers, equipment suppliers and over thirty key sub-contractors. In the process, says Bob Milne, the firm has seen major shifts in its competencies, what he describes as:

- From technical and data focused *to* management and leadership focused
- From functionally focused *to* process focused
- From task management focused *to* relationship manage-ment focused

Almost tripling their turnover in the process, Hooker Cockram have gone from a firm that just built things to one that manages the construction process from feasibility planning to final hand-over. Outsourcing to the best in the business brought the skills and the impetus to make it happen.

As managing director of Hooker Cockram, Bob Milne's experience at taking a tradition-bound business and chang-ing its vision is second to none. Here he explains some of the learning that he has had in developing a truly outsourced network, without the benefit of a clean sheet of paper.

Asked what were the driving forces behind the firm's deci-sion to change he notes that 'it all comes back to the issue of customer focus. When we ran customer focus programmes in the company some years ago, it became apparent that many of our key clients wanted us to provide a service that:

- Embraced all stages of the project delivery process
- Ensured high-quality outcomes – both design quality and construction quality
- Provided a very high level of service throughout the entire process – particularly to the forecasting of project finan-cial outcomes.'

A suitable case for outsourcing

Milne explains, 'The way we could see to achieve these goals was to focus on "management of the process", and secure the best designers and contractors that we could, operating under our umbrella. This then led to extending the use of out-sourced contractors into the pre- and post-construction phases of the contract delivery process; by outsourcing the work to architects, process designers, validation experts and so on. This became a process where we could gain a real competitive advantage by accessing leading-edge profes-sionals in each field. Each of these professionals then added to the network we were establishing and gave it real size.'

The toughest part of the change process for Hooker Cockram came early on recalls Milne. 'We have seen the enemy and he is us! encapsulates the issue,' he says. 'The greatest barrier we had to overcome was in achieving a col-lective mind-set shift at board level. Our chairman's input and vision at that stage was of enormous help, as he helped us open our eyes to the possibilities that could occur if we made a major shift in our thinking.' He adds, 'At the time we were starting to move, a savage recession hit the Australian con-struction industry, and we had to apply some severe surgery to the company to ensure our survival. While this created an initial setback to our plans, it also provided an opportunity to recruit a new breed of people and mould them in a different way to enable us to achieve our new goals.'

One of the greatest problems for Hooker Cockram has been in getting the balance right between what many of the team would like and the financial realities of a project. Says Milne, 'One of the greatest discoveries we have made is the need for empathetic facilitation skills in our project leaders, particularly during the design phase of projects. The tradi-tional hard-nosed contractor approach does not bring out the best in the design team, many of whom are by nature cre-ative, sensitive technicians who respond very well to a helpful, encouraging leader, rather than one who is purely a driver. The real art is in finding the correct balance, as there is still an imperative to adhere to time, cost and quality goals, which are often set very high. To avoid these problems we are now much more careful about our selection and recruit-ment process, employing psychological profiling to identify incompatible personality and behavioural traits and avoid employing people who do not exhibit appropriate personali-ties and behaviours.'

Outsourcing

Finally, Bob Milne shares his experiences of choosing the right sort of outsourcing partner. 'We find that we quickly identify the long-term supplier/partner from the once-off contractor, because it is obvious very early in the relationship if the culture of the supplier organization is or is not aligned with ours. We need our providers to have a culture that is customer focused, values long-term relationships, is not avaricious and rates quality outcomes as extremely important.'

Milne continues with a good piece of advice for any potential outsourcer to keep at the front of their mind. 'Technical competence and excellence, combined with financial competitiveness are merely seen as a necessary prerequisite to getting "an invitation to the dance". We do use some evaluation criteria to select suppliers in the first case, these being based on models developed in Australia by the Construction Industry Development Agency, but generally they are quantitative methods of satisfying the issues outlined above.'

FoodSaver saved by the outsourcer

Outsourcing for success can take on many different forms – this shows what getting the right marketing help can achieve.

A product called FoodSaver, developed to extend the shelf-life of fresh food, was heading into big trouble. Despite the fact that the idea was completely relevant to today's food retailing, creators Landmark Products just couldn't get it sold – hours of frustrated marketing effort came to nought. That's when they hit on the idea of outsourcing – making the sell someone else's problem. Enter Stephanie Schuss, a marketing consultant specialized in launching new products on home-shopping channels. Says FoodSaver's CEO, 'we used Stephanie's ability and relationships to save time, money, plus the frustration of getting to the buyers. We cut the sales cycle down by two or three months – we went out and outsourced the skills and the know-how we needed to make that product work.'

Chi-Chi's International – a model of outsourcing excellence

Begun in the USA in 1977, Chi-Chi's is the world leader in the Mexican dinnerhouse restaurant segment. Chi-Chi's International (CCI) was started as an independent entity in 1988, to develop the concept world-wide (outside the USA and Canada).

The company's strategy is to provide a festive, fun, family restaurant experience coupled with fresh, tasteful products at reasonable prices served by friendly helpful staff. This strategy has had proven wide appeal, not limited to particular cultures or companies. Currently Chi-Chi's International operates in Europe, North Africa, the Middle East and Asia, through wholly owned and franchised units in Indonesia, Kuwait, Luxembourg, France, Germany, Belgium, the UK, Spain, Tunisia and the United Arab Emirates.

CCI operate two types of restaurant: the original Chi-Chi's Mexican Restaurante concept, designed for a casual dining Mexican theme experience in an area from 400 to 800 square metres; and a Chi-Chi's Cantina/Grill – a 1990s evolution of the Chi-Chi's concept, designed to appeal to a wide range of guests including young singles and couples in an area from 250 to 400 square metres. CCI development is based on granting a licence for multi-unit development in a specific geographic area, usually a country or state. From their corporate headquarters in Brussels, Belgium, CCI through a wide outsourced network provide:

- ■ Equipment requirements
- ■ Approved product suppliers
- ■ Development of local suppliers
- ■ Training of executive management
- ■ Marketing support
- ■ Average product usage and costs
- ■ Construction plans (prototype plans if required)

Individual restaurant projects are supported by CCI's in-house professional staff to provide the training and assistance necessary for opening and operating a CCI franchise. This includes:

Outsourcing

- Site approvals
- Planning review
- Final plan and decor approval
- Operations manuals
- Training of restaurant managers
- Crew training
- Pre- and post-opening support

Ongoing development and operational input is provided by a support staff of franchise consultants, each with specific areas of responsibility for training, R&D, equipment and marketing – all of it outsourced from Brussels. Everything from new product design, food and catering supplies, transport and logistics, even marketing is outsourced to carefully chosen suppliers with whom CCI has developed close partnership links over a lengthy period of time.

CCI's founder, Terry Smith, says that close attention to detail and the creation of systems and processes that work around the world prove that 'CCI has crossed language and cultural barriers without noticeable differences in products, menu assortment or customer response.' Gnawing on a nacho in Bali, feeding on a fajita in Frankfurt or drinking a margarita in Madrid, the one thing the customers don't know is that wherever they go, the food and the drinks are not just the same on the menu, they all come from the same places around the world. CCI is one of the most totally outsourced businesses anywhere. Supplying goods, services, ideas and a lot of marketing support to over thirty restaurants scattered around the world could seem to be a nightmare, to Terry Smith it's just a usual business day. In fact he is so outsourced – with only seven people in the Brussels headquarters – that his job and the job of his other key people isn't day-to-day operations but business development.

Terry Smith began searching for the 'very best and the very brightest' in 1988. As an international food consultant, with a background in restaurant operations as well, he knew a lot of people and he knew those that were good. His in-house operation is tiny. One person looks after legal issues as, 'contracts are the most important thing we deal with, as well as deals with potential franchisees'. A head of operations oversees plans, equipment requirements, internal layouts and opening details – external suppliers support the process. A head of training trains the managers and the

A suitable case for outsourcing

employees. Current employees and management staff with good experience are used to train new employees. Managers from Belgian operations are seconded to Kuwait and Jakarta for weeks of intensive training of local staffs: 'a great added incentive' says Smith, who points out that virtually all the people they have hired as CCI has grown are still with the company.

CCI even outsource all their marketing and promotions. 'I wanted the best there is in our business,' says Smith, 'and I couldn't persuade him to join us, so we outsource to his firm instead'. CCI doesn't use the marketing consultancy for anything corporate, 'I tell them that we are not interested in promoting our image, or getting people to spend more, all we want from their promotional efforts are guest-count increases.' On this basis the marketing consultants create and plan four major promotions each year, which go worldwide. 'They can fit them into the local market, add their own words, but we provide most of the materials from a central point,' says Smith.

Smith says that one of the great advantages of outsourcing marketing is that you get 'outside input and someone who thinks about us'. Are there any downsides, like confidentiality? 'Not really,' he says, 'we are loyal to our suppliers, we are not going to go out and test the market for better offers every six months. On the other hand, they have to appreciate that we are in a price-sensitive business. Remember, we want them to be successful too.'

Smith points out that having suppliers that work with others can be a boon to business. When our marketing consultancy was asked to work for another chain [Chez Leon, that sell the Belgian mussels and chips experience on a franchise], he asked us if he could. Now we work with that chain as well sharing ideas and sharing transport in some cases.

At restaurant openings, Smith and his team hire local promotional agency support 'who develop with us the plans for the opening, so we get lots of press coverage in advance. We tell them the message we want to get across and ask them to refine it and fit it for the local market.'

CCI hasn't changed its main suppliers since it began and it helps a lot, as 'they become part of your business and make a real contribution. they come and eat in our restaurants, they tell us what is happening in the business, they always have lots of new ideas.'

Outsourcing

Initially – until they created their seventh restaurant – CCI handled its own distribution, 'but it was eating up our people's time and causing internal conflict as well,' remembers Terry Smith. Now everything is not only shipped by outsourced service, it is warehoused as well. Apart from spot quality checks, although they have also outsourced a lot of that too, CCI don't see the product unless they visit a site. Even test kitchens for new products are not their own. When working on new menu items and working up spices and rubs for flavour they use outside food chemists 'who are a lot better and a lot better equipped than we would ever be'.

A sizzling chicken fajita in a CCI outlet anywhere in the world provides a good example. The spices in which it will be marinated are produced by a specialist external supplier to exact specifications. These are shipped to a facility in France, where an Irish company – the largest chicken producer in Europe – forms the spice pack into a marinade. Exactly 15 grams of marinade (CCI's own proprietary recipe) is injected into the chicken pack. The chicken breasts are all exactly the same size and weight, meaning that cooking instructions wherever you are at a CCI facility never vary. 'It's total replication,' says Smith,' we totally control quality, our job is to ensure that the flavour is constant.'

Stone-ground tortillas are shipped in bulk from the best processor in the USA and held in the outsourced transport firm's warehouses – it is up to them to work out how materials get to the different locations. 'We get stock reports each week from our distribution company,' says Smith, 'so we constantly know what items are moving. If an item is moving faster than expected the restaurant calls our distribution consultant and we look at options.'

Operating at great distances can bring supply problems, but CCI has a local crisis management programme just in case. 'We have a local emergency supplier for every product, where possible, and each restaurant carries the formulas for our spice packs just in case,' points out Smith,' but normally we are able to control the stock. I only get involved about five times each year.'

For a business start-up, albeit with global ambitions, cash-flow is always the crunch. Smith solved a lot of his problems by pushing the cost of product on to the distributor – who actually owns CCI's materials. 'If I order from the USA I am probably putting up $60 000–70 000 a container. Now my

A suitable case for outsourcing

distributor is responsible for paying upfront for the product, the wastage, the custom controls, the shipping.'

With a mainly cash business at the customer end and 30 days' payment terms, CCI can have sold the product four times over before they have to pay out. Add to that four weeks to ship from USA and that adds four more weeks before all the product is sold. On that basis they gain eight weeks of cashflow. 'In a business like ours that makes a lot of difference,' notes Smith.

How does the distributor feel? 'By giving him ownership of the problem I've also gained a partner and one who can give me lots of information, advice and ideas on prospective new suppliers as well. What we've got is a partner who excels at his core business, just as we try to excel at ours.'

Smith, who can't understand why other businesses don't head in the same direction, is a total supporter of outsourcing both at a tactical and strategic level. He is using it to keep costs down – not cut costs – and he is using it at the very core of his business.

When he started working with his logistics and distribution outsourcer he said it took him a year 'to train them to do it our way, but now they get better and better at what they do, better than we ever could. We put their managers into our training programmes, so when they go out to buy they know what we want. Often they bring new suppliers back to work with us.' He adds, 'by doing all this, we keep the prices down with them and we make sure that those prices are lower than our franchisees could get anywhere else.'

Terry Smith says that partnering for outsourcing requires any organization to have a very good idea of what it is and what it wants to do, then it has to be obsessive about getting there. Saying that 'you have to be in control', Smith suggests any potential outsourcer consider the following carefully:

- Ensure you have the same or a superior product
- Train suppliers your way – get what *you* want
- Understand that it requires constant communication
- Get them knowledgeable about your business, so they can contribute to it and add value
- Keep thinking not just where can I add the most value but can a supplier add more than we can?

Smiths says 'Constantly asking yourself which part of the

Outsourcing

value chain you should be in and which parts you should get out of is the key to successful outsourcing. But be warned it doesn't stay static for long. In our case what we do best is control.

- ■ We control training
- ■ We control quality – through an approved list of suppliers
- ■ We control restaurant standards
- ■ We control use of the brand – from the sign out front to the decor
- ■ And we control the follow-up training and ideas and that never stops'

Setting those standards before you get into relationships is vital, Smith believes. Asked does it really matter if every tortilla and every piece of chicken comes from the same place, he points out that it's not just so that the customers will get what they have come to expect. 'We need a high standard for all our products. If you don't set a standard the tendency of the franchisee is to buy cheapest, not best. So if you don't have that high standard you will ultimately start sinking fast!'

Good advice from a high priest of outsourcing – take heed before you get out there!

Gardner Merchant

Gardner Merchant (GM) is the UK and Europe's leading contract caterer, serving two million customers a day in 6500 outlets world-wide. Its alliance with French caterer Sodexho forms one of the world's leading supplier of contract catering services. GM employs 55 000 people in Australia, Belgium, China, France, Germany, Holland, Hong Kong, Ireland, Japan, Kazakhstan, Malaysia, Russia, Singapore, Spain, United Arab Emirates, the United Kingdom, and the United States of America.

David Ford is GM's Chief Executive of the UK business. Here he talks about the current outsourcing picture in the UK, Europe and the USA from the client and contractor perspective.

A suitable case for outsourcing

1 Typically, who is responsible for outsourcing? Is it a variety of people depending on the area of operations or are there outsourcing vice-presidents appearing on corporate pay-rolls? For example, there is currently talk of creating a 'chief resourcing officer' (CRO) as an operational role.

As a contractor we have seen our client contacts change as our business has evolved. Post-war, contract catering was considered part of statutory staff welfare packages, putting it under the responsibility of the personnel director. Today contract catering and facilities management are modem market-driven businesses. The sophistication of client contracts makes them more likely to be the responsibility of the finance director or another purchasing specialist.

2 Is the whole question of outsourcing something that the CEO needs to champion?

The move to an outsourced strategy is a very significant one which often involves the scrutiny and possible redefinition of the company's core business. By their nature such decisions must be the property of the chief executive. When British Aerospace (BAe) decided to outsource all its catering services to Gardner Merchant it was part of a decision about the company's strategic direction taken at chief executive level.

3 What areas can be outsourced and why?

Like other areas of best management practice outsourcing is not restricted to certain areas. It is a strategic move to focus on core business skills – skills which have created competitive edge and success – while simultaneously benefiting from expertise in non-core areas. BAe realized that GM could provide benefits for its employees which it could not provide itself – for example, by creating a career ladder for its employees, GM can motivate and reward its staff in ways which are not possible for BAe. BAe also recognized the benefit of GM's research and development resource, specialist IT systems and health and hygiene expertise.

4. Where have there been most successes with outsourcing? What areas respond most readily to this sort of initiative? Where have there been the least successes? What areas or industries respond poorly to outsourcing arrangements?

There are no hard and fast rules about which industries respond most positively to outsourcing. It is more useful to talk about characteristics rather than sector or industries when identifying successful outsourcing companies. 'A

Outsourcing

willing buyer and a willing seller' is a good start for any outsourcing arrangement.

Companies who see outsourcing as a panacea for all ills are likely to be unsatisfied. Some companies believe that outsourcing is a way of exporting operational or managerial problems. This can result in the contracting out of poorly defined functional departments with expectations of the contractor finding quick-fix solutions which may not exist.

Overemphasis on cost is another warning sign. Proper partnering where companies both prosper from an outsourcing arrangement is a good deal more sophisticated than a lowest-cost selection. The ability to recognize the mutual benefit of sharing expertise and resources is a key element of any deal.

The introduction of compulsory competitive tendering in the UK public sector demands that all outsourcing decisions were based on lowest cost. Such legislation makes best-practice outsourcing deals impossible to complete.

Companies which outsource the management of a department or process in a piecemeal fashion are unlikely to succeed. Contractors must be regarded as experts who are able to manage whole operational dynamics. A company which sets a contractor goals but demands control over elements of the outsourced function cannot expect to realize the full benefits of the partnership.

5 How do you maintain quality and other standards in an outsourced organization?

Problems with quality only arise when a company is unsure why it is choosing an outsourcing strategy. As long as clear goals and objectives are shared and understood by outsourcing partners and regular quality checks are agreed upon problems should not occur.

6 In terms of creating relationships with others (both individuals and organizations) who act as suppliers/partners to you, how do you go about choosing them? Are there any particular criteria, before or after the fact measurement systems to use?

When choosing a new partner there is a minimum level of investigation which should be completed. Use as many resources as possible. Talking to other clients of contractors is one of the quickest ways of evaluating the likely quality of service delivery. At GM we encourage prospective partners

A suitable case for outsourcing

to do this and, if possible, to visit other client sites where we operate.

Meet the people. Although a sales representative can provide valuable information about a contractor it is important to meet the staff who will be working on the business day-to-day.

Walk the halls. Visiting the site of a prospective future partner and examining its operations is a vital step in understanding the value it will bring to an outsourcing deal.

7 Do you feel that it is US corporations that are pioneering outsourcing around the globe?

There is a good deal of confusion between quality and quantity when comparing UK and US outsourcing. Although there is a much higher penetration of outsourcing in the USA (in the USA 80 per cent of all catering contracts are outsourced compared to 40 per cent in the UK) the level of ingenuity is similar on both sides of the Atlantic. In fact, it could be argued that the more challenging UK commercial environment demands a greater level of sophistication than the USA.

The UK catering industry stems from a post-war welfare mentality when the provision of food for the workforces was a statutory requirement. Since that time the industry has undergone massive changes, but it, still suffers from the hangover of a 'gruel mentality'. No such mindset exists in the USA. While the US customer is happy to pay a commercial tariff for 'in-house' catering services the UK customer still expects such services to be significantly cheaper than high-street restaurants or bars.

The UK catering industry is closely involved with and influenced by the changes occurring in the state-owned public sector. For many the introduction of private contractors to the public sector and its gradual deconstruction are one and the same process. Contract wins in the public sector can come wrapped in emotive and complicated political arguments where the nature of the service is largely irrelevant. The successful contractor can find itself the brunt of considerable political bad feeling resulting in internal ideological factions and sour employee relations. This is in contrast to the USA where the catering industry is less shackled by political machinations.

There are also practical differences. For instance, the premium value placed on space in this country plus an older

Outsourcing

estate means that the facilities which are outsourced are often in a worse condition than the USA.

The size of the USA means raw materials are plentiful all year round. In the UK and Europe shortages can create considerable price fluctuations which can hit the bottom line hard.

8 Do you feel that some organizations – just as they are now saying that downsizing has gone too far – feel they have off-loaded too many of their operations?

Downsizing and outsourcing are sometimes confused because it is presumed that the objective of both processes is to reduce the headcount. At GM we have three broad objectives against which the success of any outsourcing deal is measured.

1 To delight customers by providing a better service than that which exists.
2 To provide a fair level of remuneration for the people that work on the business.
3 To be reasonably rewarded for doing so.

It would be untrue to say that outsourcing never results in a reduced workforce. However, it should never be a main objective.

9 If so will there be a reverse trend of insourcing parts of the organization all over again?

Outsourcing arrangements which are the result of well-considered strategic planning and a recognition of partnering benefits are examples of best management practice, not management fads. Such deals offer value to an organization which it cannot realize alone. The 'insourcing' of functions would suggest that the company's original decision to outsource was poorly thought out or a change in market conditions had occurred.

10 Finally do you have any anecdotes or quirky experiences?

GM's business is varied and far-flung. We employ more than 55 000 people in twenty countries, the vast majority of which work in groups of five people than less. The very core of our business is the ability to manage a massive scattered workforce. Our clients recognize this and often call on us to do more than just prepare food. For instance, in the UK more than one-third of our contracts are to supply more than just catering services.

After the Falklands war in 1982, the British Ministry of Defence (MoD) asked us to become involved in a project to reconstruct the islands. Our remit was a full life-support role for the members of Her Majesty's forces and other contractors rebuilding the war-torn islands supplying everything from low-end hotel services though to dental and medical care.

Although morbid, the extent of our duties is probably best summed up by the one item for which we were found lacking – body bags. When a contractor suffered a fatal heart attack on the island the MoD expected us to handle the arrangements. It's to our credit that we did so without a hitch.

(interview conducted by James Cherkoff of Burson Marsteller, London)

Andersen outsources its creative core

Pioneers of professional services outsourcing (tax, accounting, benefits), Andersen Consulting took their own advice when they outsourced their complete marketing and communication's operation to Murphy & Co. in 1993. Stating that they were 'more than ready to take the risk, because we were asking our clients to do the same', Andersen said that it brought a new level of professionalism to these operations.

McKesson Corporation

McKesson Corporation, with headquarters in San Francisco, California, is a $12 billion logistics management firm. Its primary line of business is the distribution of pharmaceuticals and durable goods to independent and chain drugstores and pharmacies and to giant retailers, such as Wal-Mart Stores Inc. (Wal-Mart), and hospitals. Over 80 per cent of the products found in the typical drugstore in the USA are delivered

Outsourcing

by McKesson. The company has operations throughout North America delivering products from more than 2500 manufacturers, such as Procter & Gamble and Johnson & Johnson.

McKesson operates thirty-eight distribution centres across the USA. It owns the largest pharmaceuticals distributor in Canada and a distribution company in Mexico. McKesson is known, however, as more than a distribution company. It is a customer-oriented company constantly innovating services such as pharmacy design and discount buying options, as well as strategic uses of information technology, all to better meet the needs of its customers.

Distribution, especially on the scope and scale of McKesson's, is an extremely information-intensive business. As a result, McKesson's information warehouse is as extensive as its physical warehouses. Every transaction for every customer – inquiry, order, invoice – is recorded in this information warehouse. And the customer is the principal beneficiary. For example, McKesson provides Wal-Mart direct access to this information, allowing the retail giant to produce detailed, real-time analysis of current volumes, historical trends, and future needs. This level of sophisticated capability provided to customers like Wal-Mart enables McKesson's customers to make more cost-effective and informed purchasing decisions.

Supporting McKesson's information technology requires a large and seasoned staff of IT professionals. McKesson employs more than 500 in its IT department, 200 of whom are full-time programmers. Even with a staff of this size, as many as fifty applications development projects are typically in the queue awaiting development resources at any given time. And, of course, these new projects compete for resources required to maintain existing systems and with those required to migrate to new, more powerful technology platforms.

These competing challenges were intensifying for McKesson in 1993. Performance of the company's legacy warehouse system, based on IBM AS/400 processors, was beginning to deteriorate, with up to four or five problems a day being reported, and availability figures dipping below 50 per cent. Migration to a new UNIX environment using Pyramid software was under way. The pressure of these competing demands for resources was the primary catalyst

A suitable case for outsourcing

for McKesson's decision to selectively outsource aspects of its applications development and maintenance activities.

A Staged Approach

McKesson chose to approach outsourcing of selected applications development and maintenance activities in a measured, staged manner. In 1993 it signed a two-year contract with Keane to manage the maintenance of its legacy AS/400 applications. Keane, with a staff of four people, took over the outstanding problems, all new trouble calls, and related support and maintenance functions. Keane assumed not only direct maintenance responsibility but also the role of maintenance manager. Instead of dealing with a number of vendors involved in maintaining these systems, McKesson now had a single relationship with its maintenance manager – Keane. As a result, McKesson was able to transfer additional internal resources and, equally important, additional management attention to its migration to the new UNIX system. According to Kathy Sierra, director of applications at McKesson, 'It worked perfectly because we took the maintenance aspect off of our desk and put it on Keane's.' Although the number of problems may not have gone down, the relationships were streamlined and problem turnaround time was reduced.

In 1995, the contract was renewed and expanded to cover a wider suite of corporate applications, including financial applications, HR systems, payroll, order entry, inventory, and general management reporting. The number of Keane people involved increased to thirty. Of the thirty, twenty-two are technical support staff and the remaining eight are management and development staff. The group represents the entire applications maintenance support staff at McKesson.

The management process

A well-structured management process and clearly defined service level expectations have proven the key to McKesson's success. There are a total of thirteen McKesson applications managers, eight of whom have Keane project managers reporting to them. According to McKesson's Sierra, 'One of the keys to success is good project management.' Each month, they report on the number of problems, the number resolved, and the time it took to resolve each problem. All these factors are compared to the original level

Outsourcing

of service agreements (LSAs) established between the companies. McKesson's applications managers sign off on these monthly reports which are then reviewed and signed off by Sierra.

A measure of success

McKesson's top priority – freeing internal resources for new applications development – has been met. McKesson employees who have the needed experience, knowledge, and understanding of the company's business culture and organizational goals have been moved to development projects. A side benefit, according to McKesson's management, has been higher productivity and improved morale for these programmers. They are spending more of their time learning new technologies and developing new systems.

Outsourcing has saved McKesson approximately 10 per cent in applications maintenance costs. These savings are being used to fund new development efforts. McKesson is, in effect, able to fund more development for the same total budget dollars.

Finally, quantifiable measurements of customer satisfaction do not exist. However, informal polls by McKesson's managers indicate that satisfaction with the services provided is equal to or greater than before outsourcing.

(With the permission of the Outsourcing Institute)

The virtual golf club

Normally, you can't miss a black rock – except in the dark. But with Black Rock Ventures you are dealing with a company that's practically invisible – although it generated revenues in excess of $10 million in its first year of operation. The maker of the Killer-Bee golf driver is being hailed as a prototype of the so-called virtual corporation. 'The reason they call it virtual is that we outsource virtually everything,' says Larry Hoffer the firm's general manager.

Black Rock not only outsources production of the golf club in Asia, it also farmed out the initial design, all the marketing and media spots and other promotional activities. In addition, another organization handles order fulfilment and customer service.

So what do they do? 'We spend our time managing vendors and strategic planning,' they say – just what outsourcing is supposed to achieve for hard-pressed executives concentrating on the wrong parts of the business.

Pumping profits from outsourcing

Texaco totally restructured its distribution to its 400 UK forecourt shops by appointing Excel Logistics to provide a totally outsourced warehouse and distribution service for all non-fuel products. The decision, the first in the industry, will be boosted by Texaco's ability to buy centrally for all their sites (allowing for regional variations of taste) direct from manufacturers. Excel will deliver fresh sandwiches, milk and snacks on a daily basis from their central distribution centre, Texaco's buying team will concentrate on their relationship with manufacturers, passing on savings to the customer.

Elf Atochem North America

Elf Atochem North America is a $1.7 billion integrated chemical company. It is a wholly owned subsidiary of the French firm, Elf Atochem, which has 35 000 employees and $40 billion in revenue world-wide. The parent company operates in a diversified set of businesses, including chemicals, oil refining, marketing, health care, and personal grooming. Elf Atochem North America manufactures a wide range of chemical products, including refrigerants, chemicals used in insulation, preservatives for fruits and vegetables, and an additive for natural gas which makes it easier to detect leaks.

The business challenges facing Elf Atochem North America are not unlike those of many large and successful multinationals: global competition, need for rapid product introductions, and increasingly sophisticated and demanding customers. In addition, Elf Atochem also faced challenges unique to its industry, especially product and operational

Outsourcing

changes in response to environmental concerns. Today, firms like Elf Atochem invest hundreds of millions of dollars to develop newer, safer products and to address industry regulations that can vary not only from country to country but from locale to locale. The challenge for Elf Atochem North America is one of continuously replacing revenues from phased-out products with revenues from newer products, while staying ahead of the competition and meeting regulatory changes.

The strategic moment
For Elf Atochem North America's CEO, Robert Rubin, outsourcing selected applications development and maintenance activities was a direct response to the company's strategic business challenges. Key to meeting these challenges on the information technology level was accelerating the company's implementation of SAP – the powerful suite of business applications (accounting, manufacturing, sales, and human resources), all controllable in real-time, via a single software architecture, on a client/server platform. Outsourcing would play a necessary role in speeding Elf Atochem's SAP implementation.

The outsourcing decision had two dimensions. First, Elf Atochem North America expected to be able to turn its managerial and professional talent toward the implementation of the SAP system. Second, the selected provider was expected to act as a 'rearguard', maintaining the legacy systems with high levels of satisfaction in the company's business units.

Other options could certainly have been pursued. For example, Elf Atochem could have hired new employees for either the maintenance or the development work. However, the risk would have been a slower implementation schedule resulting from the need to handle a large influx of new employees. Then, when the project was over, the possible surplus of employees would need to be dealt with. With outsourcing, the contract would be able to address both the phase-in and phase-out periods.

The selection process
Elf Atochem North America selected Keane as its provider following a rigorous process – one which has been documented in the popular press as groundbreaking in its level of

detail and rigour of methodology. Of particular interest was Elf Atochem's decision to include actual contract language in the request for proposals (RFP), including details of expected technical and business terms for the relationship and the performance criteria that would define success. These performance criteria focused on output, quality, and cost and mirrored how Elf Atochem North America measures the success of internal support groups providing similar services. Performance guarantees against these criteria were established and supported by both financial incentives and penalties. Customer satisfaction was reflected in measures of response time, accuracy, and size of backlogs. It took approximately four months from the time the decision to pursue outsourcing was made until the completion of the RFP.

This detailed document was then sent out to a number of potential providers. About one-third chose to respond. The next step was a bidder's conference where specific questions about the proposal were raised and answered. This was followed by another round of written responses followed by company interviews. As the process proceeded, and the requirements tightened, the number of competing vendors continued to drop until there were three out of which Keane was selected.

An intangible in the selection process was flexibility on behalf of the vendor in adapting, where appropriate, its operations to those of Elf Atochem. This intangible was carefully evaluated throughout the selection process. In addition to making sure that the requirements would be met, the process also evaluated the vendor's willingness to work within the Elf Atochem North America culture.

Implementation
The actual engagement began in the autumn of 1994 and implementation took place on a business-unit-by-business-unit basis. The entire implementation covered thirteen business units comprising five business groups. Much like the RFP process, and included as part of the RFP, a schedule of implementation of the new application and corresponding timetable was presented to each business unit. In addition to being based on IT concerns, the schedule matched Elf Atochem's overall business strategy.

Personnel plans were equally important. Since not all

Outsourcing

legacy system maintenance was being outsourced, there were opportunities for some Elf Atochem employees to stay in a maintenance role instead of moving to a development role on the new systems.

Integrating the employees from both companies was also critical. Today, there is no recognizable difference between Elf Atochem North America and Keane employees. Proactive techniques, some as simple as inviting Keane employees to Elf Atochem North America holiday parties, have been used to create a one-team feeling.

The lessons learned

The results for Elf Atochem North America to date have been very positive. Most importantly, implementation of the SAP system for the first business unit was completed in just 11 months. Some of the key lessons learned by Elf Atochem's CEO have been:

- Make sure that you've paved the way inside the organization for the changes brought in with outsourcing.
- Keep your own people well informed of exactly what is being done and why.
- Pick a provider that is flexible and can adapt to your company's business.
- Similarly, listen to the new ideas brought in by the provider's team.
- Do everything possible to build bonds between the internal team and the outsourcing vendor's people.
- Recognize the need for ongoing management of the relationship.

(With the permission of the Outsourcing Institute)

It doesn't have to be big you know

Outsourcing doesn't have to be a big issue. Sometimes it pays off to think small. Consider M. S. Harman in Columbus, Ohio – they're about as small as a company can get. Harman has sales of half a million dollars a year supplying oil-cans and plastic spouts to major retailers. But the company – in reality – is just Walt Harman and his son, operating from an office over the garage of their home.

Walt handles product development and marketing and the son deals with finance and administration. Product development and packaging is contracted out, manufacturing takes place in China. Harman says that 'most companies that get into financial trouble put too much money up in the beginning and it gets swallowed by rent and maintenance. We prefer to put our money into calling on clients and communicating with them to improve our products.'

AT&T Human Resources

AT&T Human Resources, with headquarters in Greensboro, North Carolina, is the human resources information systems provider of transaction-based applications on a global scale for the $75 billion telecommunications giant, AT&T – a world leader in telecommunications and information processing. With the divestiture of AT&T into three independent companies, the role of AT&T Human Resources Information Services is changing. What was once an internal support sources apartment funded as a corporate entity is quickly becoming a service provider delivering capabilities to a family of companies through various funding methods. This change places further demands on the already challenging task of supporting the human resources information systems requirements of an organization of the size and scope of AT&T.

The reasons behind the decision to outsource
In 1994 AT&T Human Resources was required to shift resources, including headcount and budget dollars, from maintenance of existing applications to development of new

Outsourcing

systems. This move was being made as part of an overall corporate-wide strategy focused on accelerating the implementation of new technologies. A key goal of this shift was to dedicate as many internal AT&T employees as possible to new development and to fund maintenance activities at a fixed-dollar amount without associated internal headcount.

The main applications under consideration for outsourcing were legacy systems. They provide transaction processing and are used to support the ongoing human resources management activities of AT&T – including meeting its related legal and contractual obligations. Although not strategic in nature, these systems had to be maintained and kept operational and were expected to continue in production for the foreseeable future.

At the time, 72 programmers and managers were allocated to maintenance and enhancements of these legacy applications. Of these, 39 were AT&T employees and 33 were a mixture of independent consultants, supplemental staff, and contractors. The goal was to replace this entire group with a single, externally managed services contract and to transfer the 39 AT&T employees to new development work.

A pilot programme
Although AT&T Human Resources' ultimate goal was to outsource the entire applications maintenance task, the approach used was to pilot the concept on a very limited basis. As a result, the initial outsourcing engagement was for one application only.

Keane was selected as the vendor for this pilot programme because it was already supplying maintenance programmers on a supplemental staffing basis and had been involved in the application's initial development. In addition to gaining first hand exposure to outsourcing in general, a primary goal of this initial pilot was to develop AT&T Human Resources' ability to work successfully with an outside organization's methodology. Based on an almost immediate success, two more applications were added to the pilot.

At the conclusion of the pilot, a request for proposals (RFP) for all 26 applications was developed and distributed to 13 companies. Each vendor had the option of responding to the requirements for all or a subset of the applications. Eleven companies responded to the RFP – eight for all

A suitable case for outsourcing

twenty-six applications and three for a subset. Factors to be considered included price, overall approach to satisfying the requirements, applications maintenance methodologies, references, proven record of performance, and project management skills. These factors used not only as a competitive distinction among the bidders but also as a comparative tool with how AT&T Human Resources had performed the work previously.

The engagement

Work on the contract began in February 1995. The Software Maintenance Management contract consists of twenty-six legacy applications. These applications require varied skill sets: COBOL II, IEF, DB2, SQL, CSP, ADS, C, DBASE III, ORACLE, ORACLE SQL/FORMS, CICS, FOCUS, IMS-DC, MARK IV, RAMUS, and TERRADATA. Every phase of the applications' activities are part of the agreement – maintenance, enhancements, development, production and project management.

The initial contract period is for two years. Critical contract terms include a committed staff reduction from the original 72 people to 53 professionals staffed and managed by Keane, committed level of service agreements that include customer-satisfaction measures, ongoing staffing with qualified individuals, and seamless integration within the AT&T Human Resources community. This outsourcing contract also afforded AT&T Human Resources a unique opportunity in its relationship with its customers. The engagement is structured such that the outsourcer performs a designated amount of work for a set dollar amount. However, included in this arrangement is a cushion for anticipated changes or additional requirements. This cushion allows AT&T Human Resources customers to receive changes or enhancements for no additional charge by Keane to AT&T Human Resources. However, it allows AT&T Human Resources to charge – in real dollars or internal credit – its customers for these changes. So, in effect, the outsourcing of applications development and maintenance has changed from a strictly cost function to a revenue-generating function for AT&T Human Resources.

Outsourcing

Implementation

The actual implementation was managed in three stages – definition and planning, transition and implementation. In the first phase, Keane brought in a team of project leaders and supporting personnel. They interviewed the current AT&T programmers and project managers. From these interviews, initial maintenance operational procedures and level of service agreements were created as well as detailed plans for the transition phase. This definition and planning stage took approximately six weeks.

In the second stage, transition, Keane began bringing staff on-board to receive specific training and to begin the process of transferring skills to the new team. Simultaneously, the maintenance operational procedures and level of service agreements were finalized and agreed. This stage lasted approximately 16 weeks.

The final stage, implementation, occurred when the transition was complete and Keane assumed responsibility for the outsourced applications. The implementation process worked well, with Richard Puljung, AT&T Human Resources, commenting, 'It was a very smooth transition because it was really well thought out. At no time did we actually lose control.'

Benefits

AT&T Human Resources achieved its primary objective of shifting resources from maintenance activities to new development. It also reduced the equivalent headcount allocated for maintenance activities from seventy-two to fifty-three with a comparable reduction in costs of over $1 million.

There were also a number of related, but not necessarily expected, benefits of the outsourcing decision. The first of these was improved employee morale. The separation of maintenance and development activities resulted in not just improved productivity but an opportunity to better match individual skills and interests to the work. Another unexpected, but important, benefit is a higher level of customer satisfaction. AT&T Human Resources monitors customer satisfaction with its services through surveys, electronic mail, and face-to-face meetings. End users have expressed increased satisfaction as a result of quicker response times to problems and lower costs – as reflected in the end users' budget.

Finally, the success of this engagement has provided

A suitable case for outsourcing

AT&T Human Resources with the confidence and comfort level needed to expand this particular engagement and explore outsourcing in additional areas.

(With the permission of the Outsourcing Institute)

Ringing up the profits

Outsourcing is for big players too. Telecom provider BT now has over £1 billion of revenue from all corners of the world providing dedicated telecommunication links for clients around the globe. BT say that today's business organizations are a great deal clearer on what they want from outsourcing, while outsourcing providers like BT better understand the market opportunities and are more flexible in what they have to offer. Together with other telecom providers BT is gearing up to meet global needs from companies seeking intelligent, cost-effective solutions from outsourcing vendors.

Cincinnati Bell Telephone

Cincinnati Bell Telephone, headquartered in Cincinnati, Ohio, is one of the three companies that make up Cincinnati Bell, the other two being Cincinnati Bell Information Systems and MATRIXX Marketing. Cincinnati Bell Telephone has approximately $600 million in annual revenues, about half of Cincinnati Bell's total revenue, and approximately 2700 employees, about 18 per cent of Cincinnati Bell's total employment.

Cincinnati Bell Telephone provides a wide range of services, both regulated and non-regulated. Regulated services include local exchange services in the southwest Ohio, northern Kentucky, and southeast Indiana geographic areas and access and billing for long-distance carriers in its regions. Non-regulated services include voice mail, Internet access, equipment installation, and providing a clearinghouse function for private payphone companies.

Outsourcing

The challenges for Cincinnati Bell Telephone, like those facing every telecommunications company, are immense and driven by the industry's fierce competition. Two underlying drivers of change are regulatory changes and the rapid introduction of new technologies. On the regulatory front, the recently passed federal Telecommunications Reform Act has made it easier for companies to compete with Cincinnati Bell Telephone within its traditional markets, while continuing to restrict many of Cincinnati Bell's operations. Technology, on the other hand, represents a double-edged sword. On the one hand, customers are demanding more services, driving bandwidth and increasing the company's opportunities. On the other, advances in technology have made it easier for start-ups to enter the business quickly and at lower initial costs.

In 1993 Cincinnati Bell Telephone made the decision to go outside the family of Cincinnati Bell companies for applications maintenance services for its accounting applications – including cost and property accounting, general ledger, budget, inventory, and payables and for its payphone clearing-house system. Until that time, Cincinnati Bell Telephone's sister company, Cincinnati Bell Information Systems, provided applications development and maintenance for these and many other systems. Cincinnati Bell Information Systems was itself, however, refocusing its business on its main market, billing systems for the telephone industry, and determined it was not strategic to continue to provide the required services for these systems. The scope of services included both ongoing maintenance for these systems and major revisions and enhancements. At the same time, Cincinnati Bell Telephone saw this change as an opportunity to drive down the maintenance costs for these systems and reinvest the budget dollars in other areas of its operations.

The engagement

The actual outsourcing engagement with Keane began in 1993 with the contract renewable every other year. The contract value is between $ 1million and $1.3 million annually and represents between ten and twelve people. The engagement was a natural extension of a seven-year relationship between Cincinnati Bell and Keane. The flexible terms of the contract allow for renegotiation and adjustments of services based on changing requirements at any time. The benefit of this flexibility to Cincinnati Bell Telephone is that as new projects come up, the umbrella agreement between the companies describes their overall relationship. The only part that then needs to be defined and negotiated is the scope of the particular project and its associated costs.

With the awarding of the contract and its implementation, the final step was to ensure ongoing monitoring and management of the relationship and its continued success. The metrics used by Cincinnati Bell Telephone to monitor its relationship with Keane mirror those previously used for Cincinnati Bell Information Systems. They include overall costs, system availability, response times, meeting estimated dollars and schedules for enhancements, and implementation of enhancements without impacts on ongoing operations.

The benefits

According to Cincinnati Bell Telephone's Bob Coogan of Accounting and Roger Rosenberger of Information Technology, the transition has worked very well. Keane is an important member of the accounting team, helping it to provide quality service – at an equal or greater level – to its customers. Costs have been reduced between 10 and 25 per cent, partially through direct savings and partially through elimination of corporate overheads in the burden rate for the IT department. The cost–benefit ratio Is also better and productivity has been improved. Much of this is attributed to improved focus on core competencies by both Keane and Cincinnati Bell Information Systems.

Another contributing factor to the benefits of the outsourcing was the location of the Keane employees at Cincinnati Bell Telephone. Previously, the maintenance work was performed off-site at a Cincinnati Bell Information Systems facility. Having the maintenance team on-site has improved and quickened communications and provided a sense of greater control to local management.

For Cincinnati Bell Telephone the lessons learned include:

■ Lay out a good plan if you want to be successful.
■ Recognize that the objectives of outsourcing are tactical and strategic and that the benefits can reach beyond the function outsourced.

Outsourcing

- The quality of a vendor can be measured quantifiably through performance metrics and non-quantifiably through improved morale and other ways.
- Early successes can open the door for more outsourcing.

(With the permission of the Outsourcing Institute)

Xerox and Motorola in billing deal

This deal shows that even when you have an outsourcing vendor you have to continue to look for best practice – elsewhere if necessary. Mastering change is critical to Motorola, an industry leader in the cellular telephone, pager and two-way radio market world-wide. Motorola creates over a quarter of a million invoices monthly and, prior to its innovative outsourcing partnership with Xerox, had a process even they described as cumbersome and disjointed. Basically, the company's billing information would be sent daily to an off-site vendor who would output the bills on pre-printed forms and prepare them for mailing.

To get around the problems Motorola has signed an outsourcing contract with Xerox Business Services to bring together both the information processing and document services using Xerox printing solutions software for form creation. Through this integrated approach, significant breakthroughs were made possible. For example, Motorola's invoices have now been standardized and are now sorted by dollar value, so that larger invoices enter the mail stream at the earliest moment. Printing, sorting and mailing have been integrated and Motorola can now make quick changes to invoices should they be needed. This in-house, integrated approach to invoice printing and mailing which leveraged the skills and resources of both organizations reduced the cycle-time for these operations by 43 per cent in the first nine months.

Successful outsourcing experiences – a composite case study

A well-managed outsourcing arrangement allows companies to bring in expertise on an as-needed basis, or to devolve operational responsibility for IT systems and resources. Both approaches allow corporate management to concentrate on the core activities that need to be managed directly by the company and from which the company obtains its key competitive advantage.

Outsourcing is not the solution to all problems or needs, and it is a dangerous option where business disinterest or technical incompetence are the driving factors. However, well-managed outsourcing provides companies both with the opportunity to bring in expertise on an as-needed basis as discussed in the first case study below, or to devolve operational responsibility for IT systems and resources, as shown in the second. Both approaches allow a company's management to concentrate on the business's core activities that need to be managed directly by the company and from which the company obtains its key competitive advantage.

The first case study below deals with outsourcing the 'new', and discusses the birth and sustenance of a new business venture in a foods company where they needed to establish sophisticated systems and procedures to support a new business venture. The systems of the new venture had to be provided on a different cost, timescale, and logistics basis from the main corporate systems that occupied the company's systems department's time.

The second outsourcing contract discussed – 'outsourcing the old' – was a relatively conventional FM outsourcing of mainframe systems for an insurance company in the final phase of the lifecycle of its systems, with the planned closure of the IT department. However final the final phase, it had a projected business life of fifteen years to settle all likely claims.

Outsourcing

Case study 1: Outsourcing the new

Background

The first outsourcing assignment began as a business and systems feasibility study of a large food company (the company's own systems people were occupied in organizing the implementation of new corporate systems for the mature part of the business). It was quite reasonable for the director to consider outsourcing systems consultancy and the subsequent systems development and FM support as the business venture had no resources of its own. It was conceived as a fully outsourced business with fifteen distributors doing the bulk of the repetitive work. The core of the business, from which they made their profit, was organizing the buying and selling agreements with other large companies involved. They have ended up with a six-person central function doing the administration and finance, controlling a £25 million turnover business.

Their Sales and Marketing Director had already established the sales and marketing feasibility of a new business venture that the company had in mind. The initial assignment was to establish the feasibility and logistics of the systems and administration needed to run the new venture. It was recognized, because of the high volumes of business transactions involved and because this involved communication with a large number of parties throughout the UK, that modern IT was needed for information processing and communication. It was also recognized that the margins in the business were very small; even with the high volumes, the technology solution had to be a very low-cost one.

The business scheme

The new venture involved the distribution of short shelf-life food products to the sites of national catering organizations, including fast-food operators, hotels and brewery groups, and canteen operators by a UK network of fifteen otherwise independent distributors, involving 5000–10 000 deliveries a week. The company organizing the scheme did not have its own regional radial distribution network capable of delivering small loads to a large number of locations, which is why it needed to use independent regional distributors.

The scheme's systems involved:

A suitable case for outsourcing

■ Common PC-based local systems used by the regional distributors to support the order and sales interface with the local delivery points of the national catering multiples. The systems had to interface with the distributors' own manual or automated stock and order systems and with the scheme's central administration at the organizing company's offices.

■ The Unix-based central administration system handled the interface between the Regional Distributors, the National Catering Multiples offices and the third-party product suppliers, entailing sales and distributors and third-party suppliers' ledgers and service statistics.

When the initial feasibility study was carried out in 1986 it was unclear whether the scheme would be viable. The study revealed that on paper all the external factors were favourable, namely:

■ The workings of the independent distributors
■ The requirements of the target customers
■ The involvement of other companies that wanted to sell through the scheme
■ The information technology.

Similarly, most of the internal factors within the company presented no significant problems. The only question of viability was raised by, and of, the company's systems department, and that was their ability, from a resource, capability, and cultural viewpoint, to handle the requirements.

What was required of outsourcing
Low hardware and software costs
It became clear during the feasibility study that proprietary hardware systems would be prohibitive in cost. Because the average transaction value was £50 and the maximum affordable administration cost per transaction including computer technology was considered to be four per cent, the cost of the hardware had to be no more than one per cent, i.e. 50p. This meant that the company would have to exploit low-cost distributed PCs and small Unix systems, which in 1986 were an innovation and therefore a perceived risk.

Because the internal systems department had no PC or Unix experience, they were suspicious about the applicabil-

Outsourcing

ity of such solutions, and were only able to propose an internal solution based upon their own IT capability, namely the mainframe. However, because of the unreasonably high cost of the mainframe to meet the requirements, the outsourced PC/Unix solution was accepted. If an external outsourcing agent had not been used to hold the hands of the business and technical people, they would not have ventured into the resulting PC/Unix solution.

Low development cost

An outline of the system functionality was sent to six software houses specializing in bespoke PC and Unix systems. They were asked to give an estimate of costs. The costs had to be within 20 per cent of any contractual quote, based upon the scope of functionality and usability defined, to ensure that the estimates they provided were realistic.

The internal systems department was also asked to estimate its costs for doing the job. It did so on the basis of recent internal mainframe projects, even though these had not been a success, incurring significant cost and timescale overruns. Not only was the internal cost estimate five to ten times larger than those of the software houses, the internal department also disbelieved the estimates of the software houses, saying that any subsequent quotes from the software houses would be closer to its own figures, which, of course, they were not. The chosen software house's quote was lower than its estimate.

If outsourcing had not been allowed, the cost of systems development would have killed the business venture before it got off the drawing board.

Short development timescales

Development and enhancement of the system had to be very rapid. Many business projects in the past and still today are held back by the slowness of systems development and implementation, even with packaged solutions. From the point the decision was made to move forward with the business pilot, the business was ready to start the pilot within twelve weeks of the go-ahead. It was felt that this was not an inappropriate timescale for the development of the initial systems so long as everybody was prepared and the right tools and people were involved.

The project involved the selection of the most appropriate

A suitable case for outsourcing

tools to do the job and the use of people experienced in their application. Outsourcing meant that the organization did not have to use the existing inappropriate development tools or to develop the skills of the in-house department.

It is amazing that companies still develop their own systems. It's rather like trying to have a barbecue: you struggle to do the job, because although you've got the resource (the charcoal) you never seem to have the capability until the job is complete – the coals always glow very hot as soon as you have finished! If you could only develop the system a second time.

All the software houses were approached because of their proven ability to use 4GLs for the development of sophisticated business application systems. The selected house and team were able to demonstrate their capability on recent assignments and the company was assured that the people it saw would be the people it got.

The 'required' system, not just the 'specified' system
The system was developed by the selected software house against a relatively detailed functional specification to a fixed price. The development process allowed the software house to exploit the features of its language as long as it did not compromise the functionality of the system.

Because the development process built in an element of flexibility, to the benefit of the software house, there was the reciprocal benefit to the business of usability trials. In these, the system was delivered to the business at an embryonic stage and checked out from a usability viewpoint. This enabled the business people to make sure the specification had been understood and that their requirements were met without misinterpretation of the specification by the software house.

Recent experiences within the company suggested that in-house development would have involved escalation of costs and timescales and a rigidity of development method that would not have allowed the users to see and comment on the system until it was finished. The users would have got the 'specified system', not the 'required system'.

No on-going 'IT' overheads
The Sales and Marketing Director did not want to commit to IT with uncontrollable overheads. While he was prepared to

Outsourcing

be advised by the internal systems department on methods and approach, including quality assurance, he did not want to build in any non-contributing overheads.

The company was accustomed to the large IT costs included in head office overheads. It was accepted that one third of the IT costs were not attributable to the delivery of any specific business system or service. They included technical and managerial people that were on hand should they be needed.

By outsourcing, the Sales and Marketing Director felt that he would be able to buy what services the business needed when it needed them, by the hour or the day, and to step up and down the level of resource to meet the variable business demands.

High adaptability and response to demand

Systems had to be adaptable as the working of the scheme evolved. The variety of pricing, charging, debt collection, and distributor reimbursement methods have grown each year as the scheme has had to adapt to the requirements of all the parties involved in a highly volatile marketplace.

Because the system was outsourced and remained FMed, a specific budget existed under the control of business management to adapt the system. As soon as there was a need for enhancement to the system, there was a response by the service provider.

In-house systems are usually subject to a communal budget and an allocation of a fixed resource, requiring work on different systems to be scheduled in advance. Similarly, IS management attention has to be rationed, limiting the rate of IT-enabled change, and typically denying attention to 'non-core' systems.

Quality – reliability and accountability

Because the systems were distributed, they had to be very reliable. Visits to the distributors in Scotland, Newcastle, and Cornwall to sort out technical problems were out of the question.

Over the years, quality has been of paramount importance as the system has evolved. The good quality of the software has been built into the evolving system because the company that supports the implementation and use of the system does so on a fixed-price contract for all changes and support.

Again, the benefits of outsourcing should be improved quality and therefore improved costs and service, because there is clear accountability for the resolution of problems. The quality of in-house developed systems usually deteriorates because of a lack of management interest in 'old' systems and a lack of mechanisms within the company to reprimand individuals responsible for poor quality, or IT management who allow mistakes to happen.

No IT/business gap

While software was key to the effective running of the new business, equally important were the business procedures and disciplines that surrounded the use of the software. The scheme had to be conceived in total. Nobody could afford a gap between the technology and its business use. The systems functionality and business procedures needed to be thought out together and had to be seamless to the business users.

The skills needed to achieve this are few and far between and can be acquired only by looking far and wide for suitable staff. Such skills as exist in the client company tend to be well used and are not willingly offered internally within a company for such projects.

Managing the risks of outsourcing

Since 1986 there have been no nasty surprises with this particular outsourced system. However, there could have been, and there may still be in years to come. With this in mind, a number of measures have been considered to minimize the risk of outsourcing. These are examined in detail below.

Continuity of mutual dependence

It has been in the interest of both parties to operate together. The systems provide a moderate continuous income for support and enhancement of the system to the service provider. If the system had no prospect of growth or change, then, with little revenue coming in, the interest to the service company would reduce and the ability of the service company to have the skills needed by the client would be diminished.

Outsourcing

Guarantee of good software practice by the service provider
It is crucial that the service provider employs recognized good practice in controlling the development, testing, and issue of software. There are many service providers who have had the best intentions, but because of an innate lack of software management skills have failed themselves and so failed their clients.

Provision of a contingency
It is absolutely essential that a contingency plan be available in case the service provider withdraws the service. In this situation there are two main services provided: analysis and implementation, and the technical/programming service. The client has limited protection against loss of the analytical/implementation service because it is so dependent upon the skills of the people providing it. However, they have the option in the contract of being able to offer employment to the service provider's staff in the event of service discontinuity caused by the provider. The client has additional protection regarding the technical service, by maintaining a limited technical capability in PCs, Unix, and the 4GL involved, that as a backstop could organize the technical contingency.

Contracts and service level agreements
A brief contract and service level agreement was drawn up when the system was originated. It provides a basic reference point but there has never been a need for it to be referred to by either party. If there were such a need, this would indicate some fundamental problem in the relationship, where one or other party was being unreasonable.

Independent arbitration
In situations where there are problems, a brief examination can usually establish the root cause. If either party is trying to change unfairly the balance in the arrangement, an objective review by a third party should be able to re-establish the equilibrium.

Summary – satisfying the multiplicity of objectives
There are always many objectives for any project (low cost, high quality, short lead times, etc.), especially when, as in the example, there is business as well as technical uncertainty.

A suitable case for outsourcing

With such a barrier of uncertainty, the only practical option was to put together a small army of soldiers selected for the task in hand. The process of outsourcing enabled different service companies and their teams and offerings to be evaluated before the small army was officially mobilized to develop and implement the systems with no compromises accepted. The answer would have been different with the internal army.

Great care and attention was given to the multiplicity of objectives to ensure that there would be no significant compromise or disappointment to the selection of the chosen software house and the implementation consultancy who have continued to provide good service over the years.

Case study 2: Outsourcing the old

The second case study involved the outsourcing of the mainframe systems and services of an insurance underwriting company. The company concerned had become insolvent due to large existing and projected claims and a shortfall of funds to meet those claims. Consequently, it was obliged to call in an official administrator, among whose first actions was an immediate reduction in operating costs, including making redundant a large proportion of the company's IS department. The company retained a basic capability to operate and maintain its IBM 3090 mainframe, which provided virtually all the company's systems.

The company had provided its mainframe systems as a service to a number of other independent insurance underwriting companies, individually and in syndicated groups. These companies were still in business, most of them unaffected by the failure of the insolvent company that owned the systems other than being dependent upon its ability to provide the systems and the processing service.

Everybody was feeling very insecure and uncertain. Complexity surrounded the ownership of the mainframe, and of buildings, ownership and rights to use the software, and responsibility for dealing with the IT suppliers, who continued to support the running of the installation, despite non-payment of bills.

Everything seemed to be held together by invisible goodwill and cooperation between the companies and their staff. However, the reality was very different; there was in fact very limited goodwill, and instead mostly mutual fear that unless

Outsourcing

all the companies and staff involved pulled together, the whole service would be jeopardized and the companies dependent upon it would fail.

There seemed to be only one thing to fear more than becoming insolvent and being put into administration, and that was having no computer to sustain the business. The issue was not cost saving but cost elimination and transfer of responsibility to a capable supplier. This process would enable the other companies using the systems to secure their future in their own ways.

There were only three weeks in which to sort out an FM contract as the key staff had been offered conditional jobs with different prospective FM suppliers. This is not the usual method of securing FM contracts, but in this situation it was appropriate and effective.

Three FM companies had been made aware of the situation and two were preparing to compete for the business. However, no service or service level requirements had been defined or documented. Tentative proposals had been made by one of the FM companies on the basis of their review of the IT department's budgets.

Fast FMing

FM suppliers are used to client companies sorting FM deals slowly, taking months to sort out detailed SLAs with the use of competitive tendering, and resolving contractual details before the commitment is made. In this case study the larger FM company was slower in making and revising its proposals than the smaller one. If you want to organize an FM contract quickly, don't be surprised if the FM supplier finds it difficult to progress it satisfactorily.

Developing the SLAs

If you don't have an SLA in place before you negotiate an FM contract (as was the case here), there is usually a barrier to developing a practical and concise SLA while sorting out the FM deal. Internal staff who know the service being provided are motivated not to assist in defining an SLA in order to disable an outside company from FMing their service. However, two things were in the company's favour:

A suitable case for outsourcing

■ Key staff would be leaving to join different FM companies in three weeks' time. Those staff were motivated to sort out the SLAs to secure their jobs with their FM company.
■ There existed a host of previous SLA documents and contracts developed for previous clients.

Transferring the key staff
There are always two or three key staff in any installation who keep it together. The transfer of these staff is the key to ensuring continuity of service in the short and medium term. If an FM company is not going to sign them up, be circumspect while taking on other people with similar skills.

Making a fair and right decision
The decision was made within the three-week period based upon some twelve criteria. Both companies had made their proposals, though there was clearly not a level playing field. The role of FM contract advisor was not to provide a level playing field for the FM contenders. In this situation, with limited resources and time, it was to make sure that the decision made was purely and completely objective, and that the time available was used effectively to secure the best deal possible.

In the three weeks, seven versions of the SLA were produced and the contract was agreed in principle. The selected FM company took over the service.

Letting the lawyers in on the contract
Once the decision had been made, it was necessary to bring in the lawyers to finalize the contract. Even though the FM service had started, it took six weeks to secure agreement on the contract.

It is difficult to know at what point in improving contracts you reach the law of diminishing returns. In this case there was felt to be a requirement to extend the FM company's liability for the FM service beyond the value of the service contract, which was in total £750 000 a year, to £2 million, which represented the value of business risk. Issues of principle were bounced back and forward until it gelled that the client companies were prepared to pay a significant (insurance) premium to secure the extra liability.

Outsourcing

What were some of the issues? What's in it for the FM supplier?

When reviewing FM suppliers' proposals from the cost viewpoint it is not sufficient to look at their charges. The company also needs to know their cost structure and how they can gain from the economies of scale.

In this case study, the selected supplier was the lowest-cost contender and they were able to be lowest cost because their technical synergy benefits were related not just to the IBM hardware and systems software but to the specialist database and related products. The successful FM company already had the licences and staff for the non-standard database and programming language. This gave them the benefit of scale that the other FM company did not have.

Where is the synergy?

In addition to the technical synergy, the successful FM company was very familiar with the finance and insurance sectors. If your business is the manufacture of building products then your synergy with an FM supplier whose parent is a bank or chocolate company will only be a technical one. While the essence of providing an FM service is technical professionalism, business sector synergy is also attractive. In this case the synergy was complete as the selected FM supplier was interested in selling on the application system as a bureau service to other insurance underwriting companies.

Flexible and complete service and transfer of service

The successful FM supplier provided the required and flexible transfer of service as well as a flexible on-going service. The first phase involved the FM company buying the computer and running on-site for a period of three months. There was no undue haste in getting the system or staff transferred to the supplier's own data centre. During that period, they paid rent for the computer room and for the electricity. Other FM suppliers were less interested in taking responsibility for the disposal of the equipment and wanted to immediately transfer the system into their established data centres to benefit from the cost savings. The successful company decommissioned leased equipment, secured and settled outstanding software and hardware lease agreements, and sold on the client's computer when they no longer needed it.

A suitable case for outsourcing

Retaining a development capability

The FM company was keen to take over responsibility for development and full maintenance of the application systems. However, the client and the other companies using the service wanted to retain control and an element of capability and, potentially, independence in development. It would have been desirable from an accountability viewpoint for the FM company to be responsible for development work and its consequences. The SLAs and contracts were developed accordingly to establish the methods of change control and accountability for resource utilization, system testing, handover acceptance, bug fixing, and consequential systems/function poor performance/non-availability.

Avoiding additional costs

It was important that the FM costs proposed by the FM supplier were the total costs and that additional costs would not creep out of the woodwork during the contract. In relation to all service aspects, the resources and services defined related to the envisaged end point in the contract, not the start point. So, for example, the client's DASD quote took into account likely growth over the contract period plus 25 per cent.

Better operational documentation and job control

Part of the agreement was that the service provider would significantly improve the operational support documentation and operational control software. The existing documentation and software was inadequate for an external company to run the systems, relying on the availability of the key staff.

It was agreed in the SLA that the documentation would be brought up to scratch. It was also agreed that the company had the right to use the documentation and software if, at the end of the contract, service was to be transferred to another service provider.

What are the controls and contingencies?

The service level agreement and the contract provide the formal basis for control. Because a lot of effort was spent developing them, most issues had been identified, discussed, understood, and resolved. This meant that there was less chance of nasty surprises. The more time spent on

Outsourcing

developing SLAs and contracts, the less the likelihood that one will need to refer to them.

Service performance monitoring

Service performance was reported on a weekly basis and reviewed on a monthly basis, and the SLA on a three-monthly basis. The SLA documented a couple of hundred service elements, of which typically twelve needed continued monitoring and review. Half of these elements were objectively and practically measurable; others were more subjective or less practically measurable. Other service elements were reviewed on an as-needed basis.

Service failure penalties

Two key service elements were identified as being key to overall service: on-line systems availability and on-line terminal response. These were both automatically measurable. The measures were at the user end of the service, not as perceived in the computer room.

The penalties were based upon penalty points. Each penalty point incurred resulted in a five per cent reduction in service charge. Penalties were applied when on-line service availability degraded below 97 per cent or on-line response was worse than 85 per cent of responses within five seconds. Both were measured over a three-month period.

Service transfer capability

The service contract was for an initial period of two years, with the option to renew. Though the envisaged life of the business was twelve to fifteen years, the contract provided the option for the client to transfer to another service provider in the event of poor service performance. The contract provided that the FM supplier would facilitate in a number of ways the transfer of service and capability to another service provider.

Retaining the downsizing option

One thing recognized in the FM contract was that while the needs of the client's business were likely to be satisfied by the mainframe solution for the foreseeable future, the option to downsize for cost saving purposes was a possible future option. As the FM supplier's vertical market was the insurance industry and it was not just an FM supplier, it had an interest in providing downsized systems as well as providing mainframe FM services. Consequently, an open dialogue continues regarding what happens at the end of the current contract, including the downsizing option. There is every reason for a continued relationship with the client, whether with the current FM arrangement or some future downsized arrangement.

Summary
The company has secured a reliable service for itself and the other users of its systems. It has transferred the responsibility for the operational running of those systems and is now able to slim down its resources and concentrate on the 'run-off' of claims that are likely to continue for the next twelve to fifteen years.

(With permission of Xephon plc)

One-stop airport shopping

The traffic never lets up at Logan Airport, Boston, one of the busiest airports in the USA. Airlines and their passengers depend on efficiency 24 hours a day – every day. Focused on their flights, few travellers give much thought to the systems and processes contributing to their safety and comfort. But since 1978, ISS has coordinated mechanical and structural maintenance, energy services, cleaning, landscaping and conveyer systems maintenance at the terminals as well as carrying out renovations and facilitating major construction contractors. Not only Boston, by the way. ISS handles total outsourcing of facilities management at other national and international airports, most recently the newly opened airport in Brussels, capital of Europe.

ISS say that their experiences prove that outsourcing facilities management to a single contractor pays off. A spokesman said 'The obvious advantage is the efficiency of working with one company for virtually any service required at a facility. Multinational companies now expect multinational service and the success of our outsourcing relationships is an equal combination of what we do and the way we do it: that includes a focus on information technologies, training and service.'

A sunny alliance

Major UK insurance group, Sun Alliance, has passed over its total IT operations to IBM, to improve its overall service levels to customers, stay up to date with technology and changing business needs and save an estimate £60 million a year. In the move over a hundred Sun Alliance staff transferred to IBM and although numbers are expected to decrease, staff have been told they will have the opportunity of redeployment within IBM's global service business.

Ericsson in partnership with Xerox Business Services

Ericsson, with headquarters in Stockholm, employs 75 000 people in 109 countries, and is involved in every aspect of telecommunications. The group designs, manufactures, and markets systems and products for processing voice, data, image and text through public, private and strategic networks. Ericsson Ltd is the UK subsidiary and has annual sales of over £500 million with 2500 employees. From their factory in Scunthorpe they manufacture equipment for public telephone exchanges and mobile phone systems.

Xerox Business Services have been providing an on-site facilities management service at Scunthorpe since 1992, helping Ericsson manage their critical customer documentation. John Morton, Procurement Officer for Ericsson and responsible for the contract management, says of the relationship, '... our outsourcing partnership with Xerox Business Services enables us to significantly enhance the documentation we provide for our customers'.

The problem
The continual evolution and diversity of the products and their installation across a huge number of sites brings major documentation problems. Indeed, documentation is an essential part of Ericsson's product. The specification, assembly and production of customized document packs,

A suitable case for outsourcing

called 'Customer Libraries', is the responsibility of Malcolm Brader, Docware Manager, and his team of seven in the Library Service at Scunthorpe.

Most documents are A4 size text, mainly operational and maintenance manuals and function specifications. There are many flow diagrams though most are generated as text. Around five per cent of pages are large-format drawings, produced in the past on drawing boards or more recently by CAD.

To cater for all the customer sites, the hardware and software variations and document revisions, the amount of paper is increasing fast. In 1994 the company printed and distributed a staggering total of 31 million sheets of paper, equivalent to a pile of paper ten times the height of the Eiffel Tower!

Ericsson's problem is to specify the documents that must go into every 'Customer Library' for each site and then print, check and deliver the 'Customer Libraries' fast enough to keep pace with the factory output, which includes new sites and system upgrades. Customer orders come through the Sales and Marketing Department to the Library Service. Working from the order, all the documents needed for a 'Customer Library' are listed and a master copy prepared by printing a copy of every sheet needed and assembling the documents into a binder. Using each Master Library as a prototype, the requisite number of copies of a 'Customer Library' is produced.

The Library Service team would request hardcopy masters of the text and graphical documents from the world-wide central repository, held on a massive IBM mainframe database in Stockholm, which would then be assembled and transported to Scunthorpe. As the document volume increased, this became unmanageable. Bringing paper from Sweden was expensive due to high archive administration and freight costs. Typically it took six weeks to get the order back, with frequent delays, documents lost in transit or dispatched to the wrong address. An order could be 800 documents and if any were found to be missing or incomplete Malcolm recalled that a further six weeks could elapse while the order was corrected and dispatched again.

Outsourcing

The solution

The first phase of the Xerox Business Services solution was implemented in 1991 with the Document Facilities Management contract to install and run two Xerox 4090 laser printers. This allowed the master documents for each 'Customer Library' to be fetched electronically, immediately and when required via a 5270 high-speed data link with the central repository in Stockholm.

The plotting of large drawings remained a problem, and the first-phase solution was to install a Xerox Engineering Systems 8840 A1 plotter in Scunthorpe and link with the database in Sweden. Ericsson soon agreed that a better solution was to upgrade the XBS Document FM contract to include a Xerox DocuPlex system and to link that to the data line with Sweden. DocuPlex is an engineering document management system supplied by one of XBS's partners, Xerox Engineering Systems (XES), and permits the input, storage, control, dissemination and manipulation of engineering and manufacturing information. Designed as a multi-user system, it can link teams of users across departments, projects and sites. With the introduction of this equipment in 1994, drawings could now be imported electronically from Stockholm, stored permanently and managed locally within the DocuPlex.

Most drawings have been created on A0 or A1 size sheets, but the high-resolution plotters included in this solution are allowing XBS to provide these for Ericsson at A3 or A4 size. These are much easier to handle and can be included in binders with a minimum of folding.

With the DocuPlex system operational the current XBS solution now permits the Library Service to build a master library by ordering single prints of the text documents. These come electronically from Sweden over the data link and are printed on the Xerox 4090 high-speed laser printer via a local 'Barr SNA' or 'GibreGateway' interface.

Most graphics documents, mainly the multi-sheet drawings, are now located in the DocuPlex system. A paper drawing in Sweden can be scanned there and transported electronically, while paper drawings held in Scunthorpe can go into DocuPlex through the local scanner.

During the initial 21 months operation of DocuPlex, drawing storage in Scunthorpe has built up to about 80 000 drawing sheets. With all the drawings for a 'Customer

Library' built up within the DocuPlex, the sets for plotting are specified and spooled off on the Xerox 8840 or remote 8812 plotter.

The XBS Document FM Library Production Group, working from the masters provided, produced the required copies by a variety of methods, according to which is best in the circumstances. Some text documents are produced directly from the Xerox 4090 via the data link, while some master documents are simply photocopied. Repetitive work, such as long documents that need to be reproduced frequently, will have been scanned and stored within the Docutech machines, so copies are easily made every time they are needed. The Library Production Group also has access to the DocuPlex system for ordering runs of large-format drawings. Most of this equipment is in continual use to meet the production targets.

The XBS relationship with Ericsson is growing and developing into a formidable partnership with distributed copier services being added to twelve other UK locations as well as a Central Reprographics Department at the Burgess Hill site. Another innovative addition has been the establishment of Document FM representatives to manage the distributed copiers on the remote sites and a Document FM Helpdesk at Scunthorpe to cater for user queries on such subjects as service, supplies and maintenance requests.

The benefits
With the DocuPlex fully integrated into the work processes for printing the master and copies of the 'Customer Libraries', the benefits have been wide-ranging. The proof of the solution, however, lies in the results: staff have visited from Sweden to evaluate the solution and have been impressed. The documentation packs, a vital part of Ericsson's product, are now produced in three weeks instead of the ten weeks needed previously. Inevitably, the targets will get tougher still, for the company's overall target is to install RSS exchange equipment, complete with tailor-made documentation, within ten days of receiving an order.

Ericsson are committed to providing superior world class telecommunications systems and products. Concentration on software and hardware design and production is deemed vital to the core business. Provision of document production services is not core business but still an essential and impor-

Outsourcing

tant part of any complete telephony system.

Other benefits provided by the partnership with Xerox Business Services include minimum impact due to the effects of machine downtime because of rapid service response times and the back-up services provided by the national network of Document Production Centres. Maximum production volumes are achieved through the establishment of a guaranteed weekly commitment. Monthly costs are fixed allowing monthly/yearly budget costs to be known in advance, providing for improved budget management and cashflow.

The Document Management unit at Scunthorpe has a high-profile world-wide reputation within Ericsson and a recent global outsourcing strategy announcement by the President of Ericsson Business Management recommended that other Ericsson companies should 'do it as they did it in Scunthorpe'.

The future

It is recognized that much of the paper will disappear eventually, to be replaced by electronic documentation provided on CD-ROM or equivalent. Ericsson is keen to evolve toward this goal and is in discussion with XBS around the provision of a service to produce the 'Customer Libraries' on this form of media, but progress depends on customer acceptance. For the present, Ericsson produces and archives its Master Library on paper. This provides the confidence factor and is retained as the last-resort backup.

Although installed initially to support the production of 'Customer Libraries', the DocuPlex system is now being viewed as the cornerstone of a Digital Document Management strategy for the whole enterprise. The Finance Department at Scunthorpe handles all the invoicing for the whole of the UK, currently amounting to 8500 invoices a month. It keeps invoices on microfiche now, but is unhappy with quality and access. The Department needs to retain its invoices for seven years and is looking at the DocuPlex as a possible archiving system. It would need its own workstation connected by LAN to scan and register its own documents.

Production Engineering has a design facility for new products. It has a small design office running AutoCAD with a pen plotter, but at present it can take up to an hour to plot a drawing. Plans exist to link a desktop PC by LAN to the DocuPlex. Then this department will be able to store all its drawings there and plot rapidly on the Xerox 8840. A further benefit is that this office will have ready access to the company's drawing archives. At a later date the expansion will include other parts of the Scunthorpe factory with the potential to incorporate the rest of the UK and even the Ericsson world!

(With the permission of Rank Xerox)

Running with the outsourcing concept

Conceived as a fully outsourced corporation from the outset, sports shoe and apparel firm Nike shows just what you can do when you create products without the baggage of the traditional manufacturing operation.

Concentrating on four areas in-house – marketing, design, development and sourcing – everything else goes to outside contractors. According to Peter Warner of Nike in Europe, 'experience is probably the biggest key in developing the expertise to be successful at outsourcing in any company. This is because it takes years to develop the knowledge and skills to know where to go and whom to work with.' Adds Warner, 'In the apparel industry in particular, it has taken us approximately 15 years to develop and nurture our source base to one in which we know all its strengths and weaknesses.' He observes, 'As our business changes so does our source base, and keeping on top of this and altering it as needed is key. At Nike, a highly organized sourcing organization of experienced and knowledgeable people is the answer.'

Nike's experience is that it pays to hold on to your expertise when you've developed it. They keep their sourcing secrets well guarded – in-house. Says Warner, 'Nike maintains a highly organized sourcing organization by using a group of seven of our own sourcing offices that liaise with the factories all over the world, to be sure we are getting the quality levels we strive for. They are staffed with highly trained people in all of the following fields: product development, design, production scheduling, pricing, quality and other related jobs. In apparel alone, this amounts to 250-300 in-house people.' Adds Warner, 'Our liaison is our own sourcing offices. For others it's agents, but we have found through trial and error we are much better served through our own people. It's more expensive this way but we get much more in return.'

Point to remember: insourcing what you are really good at helps your outsourcing to work well.

Helping banks to save cash

Persist, a software organization in Spain, is helping local banks make considerable savings on their IT costs – and guaranteeing it too. Persist applies rigorous hard and soft technologies to reduce – significantly – the cost of maintaining systems and applications software. Offering outsourcing and insourcing solutions, they guarantee outsourcing customers 30 per cent reduction in software maintenance costs in the first year and its insourcing customers a 25 per cent increase in productivity.

Panasonic switched on to the digital future

Panasonic's Cardiff TV manufacturing facility has gained significant benefits from switching its print production from outside commercial printers to an XBS Document FM, on-demand digital print solution based on Rank Xerox's DocuTech. These include savings of over £50 000 per year through reduced wastage and system benefits and improving production lead times from 12 weeks to only two days.

For many companies, manuals are an important part of the manufacturing process to be booked into the MRP schedule well ahead of production. Indeed, for a few companies, notably producers of household goods, the production of coherent and easy-to-follow literature is integral to the

A suitable case for outsourcing

product's purchase and usage. Many consumers have little idea about operating videos, televisions and camcorders without that all-important user manual.

Panasonic's Cardiff factory, which manufactures television and microwave ovens for the European and old Eastern bloc markets, is a prime example of how to seamlessly join document production into the manufacturing process. The company produces 50 different standard models that can vary widely in specification from market to market. A model run can be from a minimum of 500 sets up to 10 000 units with a typical life cycle being two years.

Each television goes out with a registration document, guarantee card and a user manual that has been translated into a number of different European languages. The documentation has to be produced on time otherwise it holds up the whole of the manufacturing process, thus these are viewed as time–critical documents.

Prior to the introduction of an in-house on-demand publishing solution, Panasonic used outside commercial printers to produce the manuals. 'We used up to four commercial printers to produce the manuals, which were printed in black and white on semi-glossy stock. To coordinate its outside print source, the company would generate a full TV set production forecast and then a three-month MRP schedule which the printer had to adhere to. Typical lead times were 12 weeks,' comments Mike Palfrey, Senior Technical Buyer at Panasonic.

Large model mix
While long-term forecasting provides a framework for document production, Panasonic encountered a number of problems because of the large model mix and widely differing needs of each country. 'Inevitably the number of televisions coming off the line differs from the forecast. This problem is further compounded by the fact that the particular models ordered per country are in a different mix and the quantities also deviate,' adds Mike Palfrey.

The use of outside commercial printers further frustrated the company because of the lack of flexibility in updating documentation quickly. Typically, a printer needs four or five weeks' notice to print a manual, with further costs being incurred if it is at short notice or a small run.

Other drawbacks Panasonic found through the use of

Outsourcing

commercial printers were wastage and lack of inventory control. 'Panasonic used to dispose of around £30 000 of out-of-date manuals per annum because of overstocking as a result of models coming to end of their life cycle. There was considerable expense at having to do test runs of manuals because of minimum print requirements. It was also difficult to analyse the inventory, as manuals were simply printed as required with the only "back copies" being held by the printers.'

Culture of continual improvement
Part of Matsushita, the Japanese electronics giant, Panasonic is imbued with a culture of continual improvement. It was felt that there was considerable scope for bringing print production closer to the manufacturing process. The bridge for making this significant move forward was an on-demand digital print solution supplied by XBS Document FM, known as DocuTech.

DocuTech gives Panasonic an 'end-to-end' publishing solution which provides the functions of offset technology – and more – but digitally. The system comprises a high-speed, high-quality scanner, storage, cut and paste, print management and a 135-page-per-minute 600 dpi (dots per inch) laser output device, complete with on-line finishing. Panasonic's services department transfers manuals from one of its six SunSparc workstations to the digital print system via an Ethernet link. Documents are authored using Interleaf, a powerful technical publishing, graphics and document structuring tool.

This need for a new approach to print production was given an added impetus by Panasonic's success in the emerging East European markets. With an upturn in Western Europe and additional demand in the East, the Welsh factory is set to produce one million televisions in 1995. The need to produce large amounts of manuals in languages such as Russian added further challenges to an already industrious production department. 'Panasonic's success meant we had to look for a new approach to producing support documents. By switching to an in-house digital print system, we could have a print capacity which was flexible enough to meet future demand. It was also felt that it was important to bring the print facility closer to the production line,' says Mike Palfrey.

A suitable case for outsourcing

In assessing its print requirement, Panasonic chose Xerox Business Services' (XBS) Document FM Division to equip, install and manage the on-site print facility and a production back-up facility provided by XBS's Document Production Centre (DPC) at Uxbridge. A Rank Xerox DocuTech Digital Publishing System was installed at the Cardiff factory in the autumn of 1994.

Significant savings

The change to digital printing has brought many immediate benefits for Panasonic (for example, lead times and total cost of ownership). The Document FM contract has enabled significant cost saving by elimination of obsolescence and origination costs of £25 000 per annum.

Far more fundamental than cost savings has been the new work approach that digital printing has enabled. By moving the print department right next to the production line, it has been integrated into the manufacturing process. With the annual target for the production of TV sets set to rise to 1.4 million by 1996, the speed and flexibility of the DocuTech system has really been demonstrated when compared with traditional offset methods. 'One specific benefit of the digital publishing system was that the Publications Department was immediately able to produce proof prints of new or revised manuals and to check them quickly. This can be done frequently, if necessary, with none of the inconvenience, long lead times and expensive set-up costs associated with traditional means of proofing,' adds Mike Palfrey.

Another significant factor of the switch to digital printing is what Mike Palfrey calls 'design for manufacture'. With a new method of print production, the manuals could be redesigned to be extremely easy to print using the DocuTech system. Previously, one user manual had been printed containing several different languages. With an increasingly diverse number of markets, this approach became impractical so manuals are now printed individually for each country.

The change to in-house facilities management has been highly fortuitous because of the significant increases in demand for TVs that Panasonic has experienced over the last six months. With the old system of using commercial printers, there would have been substantial cost penalties for meeting extra demand and lack of flexibility to cope with additional work. Now, if there is a peak which exceeds the in-house capacity, extra work is simply printed using XBS's network of DPCs as back-up facilities.

Such is the increase in demand for manuals that Panasonic now have a second DocuTech working hard alongside the first one. 'With the second DocuTech, it further increases the Document FM's print capability as a certain per centage of machine time is spent working on documentation, rather than just printing,' says Palfrey.

Looking further ahead, Mike Palfrey can see the true globalization of the print function for Panasonic TV with the development of manufacturing sites in Japan, the USA, Malaysia, Germany and the UK all being interconnected. 'As a true world player, Matsushita has a truly world-wide approach to the manufacturing of its many electronics products. The print function should be a logical extension of this.' Thanks to the global networking capability of DocuTech this dream could become reality very quickly.

(With the permission of Rank Xerox)

Blowing up a storm

Typhoon Software have certainly created a storm in IT circles. If you outsource computing operations to them they'll whisk the work a world away – to St Petersburg in Russia to be exact. Now used as an outsource vendor by organizations as diverse as Honeywell, Novell, Harris and WordPerfect, they have become a preferred outsource of supply for many software companies around the globe.

California-based Typhoon had the idea of selling outsourced IT services from Russia when it realized just how many, high-quality programmers were available. Says Sean Watson, in charge of Typhoon's business development, 'we maintain programming facilities in St Petersburg. Our well-established relationships within Russian academic and government circles give us unique access to some of the most technically competent individuals in the world. We also have extraordinary access at the ministerial level, leading scientific institutes and academies of science.' Explaining how Typhoon operates, Watson adds, 'Russian programmers have proven themselves capable of mastering the most complex engineering and programming tasks – their skills are recognized world-wide. Typhoon's strategic combination of Western management, advanced technology and Russian programming expertise allows us to provide the highest quality programming service at the lowest possible cost.'

Two examples of Microsoft's outsourcing policy

World-wide PC software leader, Microsoft is a major outsourcer for both internal support and customer-related services. Microsoft's outsourcing policy is shaped by issues that are similar to those facing many major corporations – the need to maximize computing resources and budgets, minimize administrative overhead and maintain focus on the company's core competencies. Outsourcing contracts are based on an assessment of demonstrated service commitment, excellence and suitability of support solutions, financial stability and price. As part of its outsourcing strategy, in 1996 Microsoft signed contracts with Vanstar Corporation and ENTEX Information Services.

Vanstar will manage Microsoft's PC procurements, including delivery, set-up and installation of both PCs and peripherals. The three-year contract applies to approximately 12 500 desktops at Microsoft's domestic sites and is worth approximately $550 million. Vanstar has integrated its proprietary order management systems with Microsoft's financial control systems and has assumed full management responsibility for day-to-day operations as well as for the 100-plus Vanstar employees working on-site at Microsoft.

Microsoft chose this solution because, until their deal with Vanstar, procurement had been spread across almost 50 resellers world-wide. Like any other corporation they are seeking to reduce the number of administrative transactions while placing state-of-the-art PCs on desktops. The agreement between Microsoft and Vanstar calls for a shared-risk pricing model whereby Vanstar can benefit from reducing Microsoft's overall costs.

In a separate outsourcing deal Microsoft is outsourcing

non-strategic, standard and generic network support to ENTEX – leading PC systems integrator – while keeping in-house the strategic skills that support emerging technologies. ENTEX, which has been a service provider to Microsoft for almost a decade, has more than 300 dedicated personnel working at Microsoft locations around the world. The contract which made ENTEX the primary desktop-service provider to Microsoft is worth $50 million over three years.

Literature and Software Logistics: document services in software manufacturing

Literature and Software Logistics (LSL) is a specialist software fulfilment supplier based in Bedford, UK. It has grown consistently and powerfully from foundation in 1994 to a multi-million pound business by providing a tailored, caring and professional software manufacturing and global logistics service throughout Europe and the USA. Its mission is to be the leading supplier of software-fulfilment services delivering a quality solution to software publishers. The Managing Director, Peter Collins, describes LSL as 'hungry for success. We deliver what we say we will. We compete by flexibility of service offering, so tailor our service precisely to meet our customers' needs.'

Xerox Business Services has been providing documentation services to LSL from early in the company's life. Initially this was as one of three suppliers, all of which used the Rank Xerox DocuTech digital production printer. Paul Bigley explained the choice of production method. 'Unlike traditional print methods DocuTech suits low-volume, short-run document production. It means we can have keen prices compared with the traditional litho process. The production lead times are much shorter because we avoid set-up processes other than loading data into the DocuTech. We are also able to offer our customers much more flexibility of stock and inventory management so reducing their asset risk tremendously. There are frequently last-minute changes in the dynamic software industry, we can print on demand to capture them all.'

LSL seeks a competitive edge

LSL competes by rapid and precise response to customer requirements, ensuring a consistently high level of service. Peter Collins said, 'To give us some kind of competitive edge we have to have the flexibility and be responsive enough to deliver in a short timescale.' With three suppliers, it took LSL five days to print from the receipt of masters, and three days for reprints. He added 'The use of multiple suppliers was presenting us with problems particularly in terms of lead times. We experienced problems when jobs had to be rerun. It was doubling timescales, which was unacceptable to us, bearing in mind that we didn't understand what those problems were until the material was ready for delivery. We looked at the various options and our core skills aren't about printing, or DocuTech, or managing that process. Our skills are in the logistics business. Plus we didn't want the initial investment in leasing or buying these machines. So Stephen, our Purchasing Manager, took away the actions to go and look at the various options with our suppliers. He asked them, "how about you putting a machine near here, we will migrate all our work to you, you staff it, you support it?" '

When LSL looked at how to beat the UK market leader in software fulfilment they had to be able to offer a global service. There would have to be electronic links with customers and suppliers in all LSL's chosen countries, to facilitate simultaneous distribution of customers' products throughout the world. This would mean on-demand printing in the destination country instructed by a central point in the UK. LSL produces thousands of titles for its customers, fulfilling the demand only when the customer places the order, to ensure that the latest revisions are included and to avoid the risks of obsolescence. Because of this and the seasonal fluctuations in demand, substantial peaks and troughs in production are expected. A company like LSL needs the support of a powerful and reliable partner to cope with this variation.

LSL selects Xerox Business Services

LSL chose Xerox Business Services as a long-term partner in documentation services. Quality and cost were vital,

Outsourcing

together with resilience to cope with variations in demand and achievement of lead-time goals. LSL wanted to concentrate its management effort and funds on its core business of logistics, and leave the funding of the printing equipment to its document supplier. The experience of staff and direct access to technical support were also important to ensure that any problems with documentation sent in by customers were detected as soon as possible. The procedures adopted have been jointly developed by Xerox and LSL to ensure the highest standards and fastest responses are maintained consistently.

Xerox Business Services has established a Document Production Centre in part of LSL's facility in Bedford. LSL has first call on production time, and all demand printing is now fulfiled by Xerox Business Services. A contract is in place between Xerox Business Services and LSL covering all aspects of the service. Two DocuTech production printers have been installed in the Bedford plant, together with document-finishing equipment to meet all LSL's needs. These are owned and operated by Xerox Business Services.

Peter Collins enthused 'The business is growing in leaps and bounds. Last year we increased by 100 per cent and 400 per cent the year before that and this year will be 60 or 70 per cent on last year. Next year will be in a similar region of 60 or 70 per cent. Our business is on track, and the contract with Xerox Business Services has supported this. We achieved our printing objectives and I think the alliance we have is mutually beneficial. In essence, it immediately takes four days off our lead time. The quality is also much more in our control.'

LSL has saved time and cost while gaining flexibility and technical support. Xerox Business Services has gained a second Document Production Centre in East Anglia, to add to its existing resources in Norwich. The Bedford facility is used to provide document services to a wide range of companies in the south-east midlands and East Anglia. Capacity can be balanced across the Xerox Business Services' national network of Production Centres, so ensuring a consistently rapid response.

A suitable case for outsourcing

Forward together

Peter Collins has a clear idea of LSL's future. 'Our vision is to offer a totally integrated documentation facility to our clients. This will allow their authors to sit at their own workstation, anywhere in the world, author a document, and send it electronically to LSL to be printed at any location globally. We are working with the Documents Direct™ element of Xerox Business Services, plus the whole global Rank Xerox network. I think that having the partnership with Xerox Business Services enhances our stature and gives our customers a better service. This year we are looking to set up some form of representation in North America, and hopefully that will be linked to the Xerox global Documents Direct™ network. Through the partnership with Xerox, we are able to implement our strategy of expansion much more rapidly than we could have done alone.' Documents Direct™ is the Xerox service that sends digital documents world-wide, so saving days in distribution time.

LSL services
- Software packaging design and supply
- On-demand document production
- Multi-platform software duplication
- Assembly and warehousing
- Inventory control
- Global distribution

Aims in outsourcing
- Reduce product lead time
- Concentrate resources on core business
- Achieve flexible production capacity
- Improve product quality so providing a better service to customers and saving scrap

Reasons for choosing Xerox Business Services
- Willingness to establish a production site on LSL premises
- Global support to enable LSL expansion
- Ability to demonstrate required quality performance at desired cost
- Experienced and technically capable staff
- Financing arrangements to suit LSL needs

Outcome for LSL
- Lead time reduced by 80 per cent
- More flexible production capability

Outsourcing

- Saved cost
- More influence over product quality
- Satisfied customers
- Improved international credibility with major customers

(With the permission of Rank Xerox)

Unisys partners with BASF

Unisys has signed a $4.4 million five-year contract with BASF to provide remote systems support outsourcing services. Under the terms of the contract, Unisys will provide computer support, data network management, systems maintenance and support services – including help-desks, contingency planning and technical systems support operations. BASF selected Unisys as their outsourcing partner due to their demonstrated flexibility in meeting the changing requirements of their clients. Unisys has begun to offer outsourcing services to clients from its InfoHub, the result of a three-year world-wide consolidation of 58 Unisys data centres around the world into one centre in Minnesota.

Digital goes to the museum

Digital Equipment has taken responsibility for the outsourcing of all the IT services associated with the running and marketing of the Canadian Museum of Nature. Digital not only assumed direct responsibility for the museum's existing IT but is also creating new systems for transforming the museum's resource richness into marketable, consumable products. First projects include a national multimedia collection repository, an information clearing house on biodiversity, nature-related, video-on-demand products, an Internet home page and electronic guided tours of the museum.

Unsuccessful outsourcing experiences – a composite case study

There have been many highly publicized cases of dissatisfaction and litigation over outsourced IT services. Here we examine some all-too-frequent experiences, with first-hand, off-the-record discussion of several celebrated and less well-known case histories.

The growth of outsourcing
FM contracts and other forms of outsourcing are becoming increasingly popular. In the UK, government reforms have created a whole new market, from public utilities through health to local government, but even before the reforms there was a core of FM providers doing good business with managers of businesses of all kinds – and usually not in consultation with the IT managers.

The key driver for this trend has been dissatisfaction with the IT service. Cost is often a factor, but cost alone is seldom a sufficient reason for organizations to make such a drastic change in the acquisition of IT services. The key attractions of outsourcing are:

- Service level improvements.
- Increased responsiveness to user demand and in providing increased processing capacity.
- Increased preoccupation with back-up and disaster recovery.
- Ease of budgeting.

The promise of guaranteed performance and costs known in advance is a powerful enticement away from an in-house service which, rightly or wrongly, is perceived to be less than perfect.

Yet many FM contracts go badly wrong in exactly similar circumstances, and there have been some highly public arguments between vendors and customers. In some cases, litigation has ensued; in many more, the service has strug-

Outsourcing

gled on, satisfying neither party, until the contract could be killed off mercifully at the first opportunity.

These are lose–lose situations; neither side gains from a failed contract. By definition, both sides saw value in entering into the contract, and its failure is a loss to both sides. The causes of these failures are rooted in the lack of experience – on both sides – in three areas:

- ■ Establishing a clearly understood and practical contract
- ■ Living up to the requirements stated in the contract
- ■ Identifying discrepancies early and dealing with them in an objective way co-operatively with the other party.

The service delivery contract

The primary requirement for such cooperation is a service delivery contract in which the quality, price, volumes, and any other material factors are defined. The contract must also make provision for either side failing to meet its obligations – provisions to which both sides commit at the outset.

Such contracts do not just happen. Painstaking care is needed to ensure that the commitments are achievable, reasonable, and financially viable. The user must define requirements in a clear, unambiguous way, and the provider must define the services on offer equally clearly and unambiguously.

A major benefit from the UK government's initiatives to 'privatize' has been the growth in awareness of the wider issues surrounding outsourcing. A foundation principle of the government's market testing is that outsourcing must be based on informed and objective decision making.

Monitoring

A well-thought-out service delivery contract is not enough; performance against that contract must be monitored, to ensure that problems are recognized and addressed as early as possible. It is vital that facts, not opinions, govern the perceptions each side has about the other side's contribution to the successful operation of the contract. It is equally vital that when the facts indicate a problem, this is spotted quickly and dealt with cooperatively.

Direct Mail Department
Butterworth-Heinemann
FREEPOST
Oxford
OX2 8BR

At Butterworth-Heinemann we are determined to provide you with a quality service. To help us supply you with information on relevant titles as soon as it is possible, please fill in the form below and return using the FREEPOST facility. Thank you for your help and we look forward to hearing from you.

What title have you purchased?

Please tell us how you bought your book by ticking a box below

- ☐ **Bookshop**
- ☐ **Direct Mail from Butterworth-Heinemann**
- ☐ **Conference**
- ☐ **Other Supplier**

for office use only

Name (Please Print)

Job Title

Street

Town

County

Postcode

Country

Telephone

Company Activity

*Please arrange for me to be kept informed of other books, journals and information services on this and related subjects (*delete if not required). This information is being collected on behalf on Reed Educational & Professional Publishing Ltd and may be used to supply information about products produced within the Reed Educational & Professional Publishing Group.

**BUTTERWORTH
HEINEMANN**

A Division of Reed Educational & Professional Publishing Ltd
Registered Office, Quadrant House, The Quadrant, Sutton, Surrey, SM2 5AS.
Registered in England 3099304

A suitable case for outsourcing

Arbitration

There will inevitably be occasions when the two sides cannot agree on the interpretation of the facts. Such cases can quickly lead to acrimony and dispute. To prevent this, the contract should, at the outset, include provision for a third party to arbitrate.

This third party will act on behalf of the contract. The aim is to preserve the value of the contract by resolving issues that either or both sides may raise about the other's perform-ance of the contract. Clearly, such an arbitrator must be independent and trusted by both sides. The right time to appoint the arbitrator is when the contract is negotiated, before any performance problems materialize, and when the cost of the arbitrator can be built into the contract in an equitable way. The arbitrator needs to have some knowl-edge of the contract and access to the performance records that are produced in the monitoring process. It can be cost effective if the arbitrator also does the monitoring. This has three benefits:

- The monitoring is impartial.
- The correct data are gathered.
- The arbitrator can maintain knowledge about the con-tract, ensuring accurate and quick judgements when nec-essary.

This form of independent monitoring is also likely to uncover problems earlier, thus reducing the need for arbitration.

Partnership support

These monitoring and arbitration roles can be regarded as the support of the partnership between customer and vendor.

Sourcing support

Sourcing support is reasonably well understood: before signing a contract the customer will need to define require-ments, issue invitations to tender, judge those tenders, and negotiate terms. Experience has shown that a number of pit-falls exist here to trap the unwary or inexperienced, and inde-pendent help for some or all of these activities is often valuable.

Outsourcing

Bid support

Equally, the other side of the contract (the bidding company) may require assistance in preparing a tender, assessing its capability or costings, or establishing the controls needed to be able to guarantee performance. It may seem unlikely that the experienced FM supplier will need this help, but, increasingly, rival bidders are also tendering for contracts. In-house IT departments, threatened by the FM bid, must respond in some way, and this 'commercial' response may be seen as an effective way of competing with the predator. Management buy-outs, making IT a profit centre, and seeking additional business outside the parent company, are all frequent responses to the FM 'threat'.

However, this is an area where government initiatives are leading the way. IT departments are increasingly becoming an IT purchasing function, acquiring IT services from the most cost-effective source. In many cases this will indeed be the in-house team, but in some cases an FM supplier will be more cost effective – virtually all organizations already use BT or Mercury as an FM sub-contractor for communications, for example.

From this analysis, two facts emerge. First, FM suppliers can be a valuable resource to the enlightened IT department, not necessarily a threat. Second, in order to choose between in-house and external bids it is vital to compare like with like.

Positioning the in-house provider to compete on equal terms with the external bidders therefore has a number of benefits:

- A leaner and more effective in-house provider is stiffer competition, ensuring that whoever wins the contract gives the best possible value for money.
- The 'purchasing' functions of the IT department develop experience in contract specification and negotiation.
- The 'providing' function of the IT department becomes more commercialized. The budget becomes more attuned to demand than to artificially imposed constraints, priorities for work and resource commitment are clarified, and future IT investment decisions are tied to contracts for typically three to five years' service, giving a more sensible and manageable timeframe than the annual budget cycle.

A suitable case for outsourcing

All this requires considerable organizational development, new controls and processes, and a change in attitude and culture. However, the government reforms are forcing this to happen in local authorities, public utilities, and the NHS. In the best cases, the results have proved extremely effective.

Establishing the groundwork

This final section reproduces one of a series of guidelines developed by one of IT Service Partners' partners, Arrow. Research on behalf of NHS and local government clients led us to develop a model for purchasers and providers of IT service to follow in establishing the essential groundwork for effective outsourcing. It contains elements of both bid and sourcing support.

This guideline covers the establishment of 'market testing' – the streamlining of the IT department, the creation of a competitive tendering framework, and the development of in-house departments as services are increasingly outsourced. Perhaps the most important lessons learnt in this research were:

- Outsourcing must be well managed if it is to be of value to the customer.
- The actions required to position the customer to manage an outsourced service well will usually enable an in-house supplier to be equally good and cost effective.
- Outsourcing is a necessary part of the IT service provision function hardware, system software, and telecommunications are almost invariably outsourced already.

Guideline A1: a systematic approach to implementing market testing

Arrow's Implementation Method (AIM) is based on four proven techniques:

- It exploits past experiences of implementing market testing in a variety of organizations.
- It replicates successful techniques (Guideline A2) and seeks to avoid the worst mistakes (Guideline A3).
- It adopts best practice used in commerce and industry for purchasing activities. For example, in IT, and increasingly in other fields too, service definition and monitoring is done with service level agreements for which expertise and training is readily available.

Outsourcing

■ It is founded upon national (and international) standards for managing service quality. BS 5750 Part 1, the British standard for quality management, proved to be a valuable guide. Many organizations have established BS 5750-compliant quality management systems, but the guidelines are used successfully by many more organizations without accreditation.

AIM has four phases. Each phase leaves market testing in the next stage of maturity. The aim is to build one step at a time towards a fully commercialized purchaser/provider arrangement, consolidating at each stage to ensure that all the gains of the previous phase are secured before starting the next phase. Each phase begins with a planning step, which allows any appropriate existing processes to be incorporated into the implementation.

Phase 1: service definition

Before any individual service can be defined, its relationship with other services must be understood. Accordingly, the service definition phase is broken into two sub-phases.

Phase 1a: tasks

The objective in phase 1a is to establish the service structure – that is, to identify all the services that are purchased or provided and the purchaser and provider for each.

■ The organization's 'Business Strategy Plan' is needed – that is, a plan of the organizational and functional relationships within the organization and the services the organization provides to its client base. If this does not already exist, it should be constructed; it is invaluable in determining who should fulfil which of the organization's responsibilities to its clients.
■ Service providers then construct a business plan to determine how these services will be provided to which users.

Deliverables

This phase delivers a catalogue of all services, showing the purchaser/provider pairings for each service and the relationships between interacting or overlapping services.

A suitable case for outsourcing

Phase 1b: tasks
The tasks undertaken in phase 1b are as follows:

- Each purchaser/provider pair completes the service definition by agreeing volumes, performance levels, and price.
- The provider then establishes the monitoring tools needed to measure the agreed service levels.
- Finally, cost accounting must be available for the service providers to set realistic prices. Only when the existing services are defined and priced reasonably accurately can competitive tendering be used to seek better value. If cost accounting does not exist, it should be established at this point.

Deliverables
The deliverables of phase 1b are:

- Service level agreements
- Price list for the services.

These are the foundation of the next two phases, or, in other words, the prerequisites of competitive tendering.

Phase 2: competitive levelling
Phase 2 builds on the service definitions to create a true trading relationship between purchasers and in-house providers, now acting as trading agencies.

Phase 2: tasks
Phase 2 tasks are as follows:

- Providers identify purchasers for all their activities – in principle, anything they do that is not purchased is an overhead whose cost must be recovered in the pricing of purchased activities.
- Basic financial management methods must be established to enable the in-house providers to trade in a commercially sound manner, in order to compete on an equal footing with third-party bidders. Cost recovery (internal charging for services) provides the trading agency's income, and the revenue budget is the agency's expenditure. To trade successfully, providers need profitability information as

Outsourcing

well as income and expense projections. It may also be neces
sary to resolve some outstanding issues such as the treatmer
of depreciation, or the cost of premises.

Deliverables
The deliverables in this phase are as follows:

- The identification of purchasers for all in-house services.
- The establishment of sound commercial management for ir
  house providers.

These are prerequisites of phase 3.

Phase 3: competitive tendering
Phase 3 establishes the competitive tendering process. Failure t
prepare the in-house providers beforehand makes it possible fc
external bidders to win the contract more easily – i.e. at a highe
price.

Phase 3: tasks
In phase 3, procedures are designed and implemented for:

- The purchaser to create the invitation to tender from the SLA
- Identifying candidate suppliers and issuing the invitation t
  tender
- Evaluating and selecting the supplier
- Negotiating the contract
- Dealing with the in-house supplier if he fails to win the contrac
- Monitoring performance
- Contract review.

Deliverables
The primary deliverables of phase 3 are:

- Procedures for competitive tendering.

Phase 4: incorporation
In phase 4, the market testing process can be applied. The 'bigges
hit' (easiest, most important, least satisfactory, or most expensive
services should be addressed first.

Phase 4: tasks
Phase 4 tasks are as follows:

A suitable case for outsourcing

- The competitive tendering procedures are used on selected services to find a suitable supplier at the right price. This may cause the services to be redefined, as the performance/volume/value trade-off will change for different prices.
- The performance monitoring, change, and non-conformity processes should be in place from day one of the contract, and a contract review schedule should be planned.
- The final stage of this phase is to 'incorporate' in-house providers. As competitive tendering proceeds, it will have one of two effects on internal providers. If the internal provider wins sufficient business, he will be 'profitmaking' (i.e. he will have positive cash flow). If he cannot win sufficient business, he will be 'lossmaking' (negative cash flow).

Profit-making business units

There are a number of options for incorporating viable business units. They can be incorporated as a limited company, owned by the organization, the management or staff, or a third-party company. Alternatively, they can remain a department of the organization.

Discussion of the relative merits of each of these is beyond the scope of this guideline, but the purpose of phase 4 is to make this decision and implement the chosen solution. It is vital, however, that phases 1 and 2 be completed first, or the provider will not be financially strong enough, and the almost inevitable result will be third-party takeover. Conversely, our approach enables viable business units to seek business beyond the organization, if its owners decide that is desirable. This can benefit the organization financially, and it also helps to ensure the long-term survival of the provider and his services at a low price.

Loss-making business units

A major benefit of our approach to market testing is that it leaves the organization free to decide how to handle in-house providers that are not financially viable. Without these preparatory phases, competitive tendering not only stacks the odds against in-house providers; it also leaves little scope to rescue them even though this may be in the organization's best interests.

Outsourcing

The key issue in resolving non-viable providers is the remaining services they provide. If the provider is to be 'liquidated', alternative suppliers must first be found, or the services discontinued with the agreement of the purchasers. If the replacement of these services will cost more than the 'loss' being incurred by the provider, the existing price is below market. The organization may choose to subsidize the provider, either by allowing him to charge up to the market rate for the services or by absorbing some of his costs as an overhead. (The cost accounting for this must be sophisticated enough to ensure that future tenders are not skewed by this subsidy.)

Deliverables
Completion of phase 4 delivers fully 'commercialized' services. Some will be purchased from third parties, some provided by internal viable business units, and some subsidized – knowingly – by the organization or individual purchasers. In every case, however, commercial pressures will ensure that the price is never higher than the market price. In the case of the subsidized services, the price will, of course, be below market price.

(With permission of Xephon)

More factors to fuel the outsourcing debate

One of the criticisms of outsourcing is the possible effects of what some observers call the horror of the hollow corporation. In this nightmare scenario, senior managers turn round one day and find out that there's nothing left in the company at all, no people, no technology, no ideas – they've outsourced everything. However, although there are cases where companies appear to have outsourced the core business – usually because they didn't know what it was – and kept the dross, much of this has been exaggerated. Equally, there are a lot of futurologists out there, who suggest that the hollow corporation is the twin sister of the virtual corporation and that's where we are all headed anyway.

Let's stop at the halfway house and suggest that, while it might be sensible not to auction off the family silver for the best price you can get and see that knowledge running out the company, there is no conceivable reason why an organization needs to perform payroll and facilities management tasks in-house. Even more important, access to world-class skills on a global basis brings opportunities for growth, not just opportunities to cut back on internal investment and people.

Outsourcing has its detractors and deservedly so in some

cases. There are people making a great deal of money out of the misery of others, which you could tie an outsourcing label onto. But acted out fairly and professionally, outsourcing makes sense and should act as a booster to business.

However, I can't stress enough how important it is to be careful in every step you take. So, here's some more advice on how to make sure your outsourcing processes work, and work well.

Make sure you are satisfied

John Reddish is president of Advent Management, a management strategy firm in the USA with considerable experience in helping clients face up to the rigours of effective outsourcing. This is his view on making sure you get the best – it's called the Four Rs.

Remember, it's *your* business. Don't get bullied into agreeing things you don't want or don't need.

'High costs, inherent weaknesses or shortcomings and limited capacity are those areas where outsourcing opportunities may exist. Once you have identified one or more of these target areas, establish standards for performance which detail *roles*, *rules*, *reliability* and *results*. The goal is to acquire outsourcing partners who can satisfy your requirements and protect your profitability. After all, you are looking for a *relationship*, not a transaction.' Reddish describes reaching that relationship as follows:

- Roles: Identify who is responsible for what. Roles determine if the partnering company will act as sub-contractor, supplier or agent. Determining the right structure and getting a written agreement go a long way in preparing for a mutually profitable long-term relationship.
- Rules: They come in two phases. First, you need to set a baseline for developing rules. In other words, you determine what rules will apply and how you will establish mutual rules. Second are the rules themselves. They come much easier once the baselines are drawn. It's like playing cards – you agree to play poker and establish the 'game' with each new dealer.
- Reliability: This is about hope and trust. You hope this sub-contractor can meet your needs and you hope their performance will prove your decision a good one. Establishing an agreement brings in trust. If there is no trust, there will eventually be no relationship.

■ Results: These are the heart of the business. We each have our specialities, but we are all in business for the bottom-line. Setting up a good sub-contracting programme and managing it well increases the likelihood that good results will happen. And if there are no results, or results fail to meet expectations, there will soon be a parting of the ways.

in brief

'When executives continuously interact with the very best talent in the world, not just the best in the next office, they are considerably more likely to stay at the top of their professions.' – **Strategic Outsourcing, *The McKinsey Quarterly, 1995 Number 1***

Going on from there, the Outsourcing Institute have come up with three warning signs that they say any potential outsourcer should heed and carefully think through *before* they begin the process of finding and negotiating with vendors. The three areas to watch out for are:

1 The process becomes dominated by financial and legal considerations or dominant vendor demands
2 Vendors have not been pre-qualified on references, reputation or existing relationships
3 Short-term benefits dominate as decision factors

Warning sign 1: Finance and legal considerations or vendors dominate the purchasing process
The most striking differences here are in the significantly higher level of involvement reported for finance, legal considerations and vendors in unsuccessful outsourcing cases. This supports the premise that outsourcing is, after all, a strategic business decision which must be made by the *business* managers. Finance and legal considerations have to play a critical role in supporting these managers, but our experience suggests that these issues should not dominate

Outsourcing

the discussions. If they do the risk is that the real business objectives may get lost in the details of the legal and financial terms of the relationship. Our research shows that a breakdown of the relationship – regardless of the cause – is an early warning sign of problems down the road.

Similarly, the relationship between the customer and the vendor must be a true partnership. Too high a level of involvement on the part of the vendors in the actual decision process is another sign. At the Institute this is most often seen in cases where the selection of vendors was made too soon, or – in the most extreme case – the vendor-of-choice was in fact chosen before the start of the selection process! This can cause the relationship to become uneven and vendor driven.

Once again, outsourcing works best, when the businesses managers:

Don't let the finance or legal considerations run your outsourcing negotiations – it's about doing business and building trust, use managers who want to do business, not write contracts.

- Drive the process, based on clear, understood, measurable objectives
- Follow a disciplined purchasing process
- Carefully build towards a win–win relationship with the ultimate vendor or vendors.

Warning sign 2: vendors not pre-qualified on references, reputation and existing relationships
The second warning sign, seen when comparing successful and unsuccessful outsourcing projects, is the relative importance placed on the various factors used to determine which vendors receive the RFP (Request for Proposals). The Institute's research shows that the lower importance placed on references, reputation and existing relationships in unsuccessful projects is striking. This adds support to the growing emphasis on pre-qualifying outsourcing vendors, based on their total capabilities, and on doing this *before* the RFP is distributed.

Don't play favourites, no matter how compelling the reason. Only ask for tenders from companies you have pre-qualified and stick to that strategy.

Purchasing experts advise not to outsource on the basis of subjective personal preferences or strictly on the basis of the lowest competitive bid. In selecting outsourcing providers, some of the important things to consider in a potential partner are:

160

More factors to fuel the outsourcing debate

- Technical expertise
- Knowledge and understanding of your company and its needs
- Management capabilities
- Physical facilities
- Human resources
- Financial strength (balance sheet and cashflow)
- Cultural fit

[These are pre-requisites for what Bob Milne of Hooker Cockram – see case study in Chapter 4 calls 'being invited to the dance'.]

As for choosing outsourcing providers on the basis of low competitive bids, any advantage is illusory. Price is only one element in total cost. Whatever is gained by low price can be more than offset by excess costs in operations and performance.

Warning sign 3: short-term benefits dominate as decision factors

The final warning sign is an overemphasis on short-term benefits as the reason for outsourcing. The problem comes about when the strategic issues are overshadowed by the need to address a short-term business issue. This does not, of course, mean that outsourcing cannot be used as a tool to solve short-term problems, it just suggests that there may be trade-offs in these situations and that the longer-term return can get compromised.

Don't oversell your management on what great service or savings you are going to get – you may be disappointed, especially in the short term.

The view of the Outsourcing Institute and their research and observations is positively backed by findings of the PA Consulting group in the UK, whose own studies parallel the US experiences. Says PA Consulting, 'The most successful outsourcers have common characteristics and demonstrate clear behaviours:

- They take a planned and systematic approach
- They manage relationships as well as contracts

Because of its generally strategic approach we refer to this behaviour as strategic sourcing.'

PA Consulting continues, 'Strategic sourcers are, in general, more satisfied than other respondents with their outsourcing activities compared with previous in-house performance. They are also more satisfied with supplier performance than the non-strategic group and have fewer unrealistic expectations. Strategic sourcers,' explain PA Consulting, 'are motivated to outsource for reasons that can benefit the wider organization. They tend to exploit a wider range of contract types, where appropriate, and they demonstrate a disposition to consider true "partnership-style" arrangements.' They go on, 'They are most likely to want to focus on their core business and take advantage of greater flexibility and cost savings – significantly. All ways in which outsourcing can benefit the wider organization. Strategic sourcers are much more likely to be letting additional contracts – in the short-term across *all* business areas. Given the correlation between benefit levels and strategic sourcing, it is perhaps not surprising that they should be enthusiastic about outsourcing and are willing to allow outsourcing closer to the corporate centre than other respondents.'

Finally, PA Consulting says that strategic sourcers recognize the importance of managing not just the contract but the relationship. To make this work, 'strategic sourcers are more willing to share risk and reward and less likely to rely on penalizing poor performance. This is in line with a greater use of partnership-type contracts, where incentives and the sharing of risk and reward are more common features.'

An excellent checklist

For the potential outsourcer, the obvious trick is to make sure from the outset that the relationship with the supplier, subcontractor or vendor is the best possible – not only from the point of view of price, but long-term considerations as well. Research and experience, it would seem, solidly confirm that taking the time to get it right and not plunging into an ill-fated relationship are the best methods.

An excellent summary of supplier selection and tender criteria is provided by the KPMG Impact programme's *Best Practice Guidelines for Outsourcing*. Entitled, Supplier Selection and Tender Lessons, it gives an extensive checklist that provides a useful guide to anyone starting out on the process.

More factors to fuel the outsourcing debate

Part one: Evaluation/negotiation

- Avoid being committed to the cheapest tender
- Establish a tender-marketing strategy before tendering – stick to it
- Tender only those companies who meet the objective criteria
- Allow the supplier scope to negotiate and show innovation, without compromising objectives
- Verify supplier claims by site visits and discussions with other customers
- Define expectations and assess the business understanding of suppliers when assessing tenders
- Request pre-tender information to check that potential suppliers can align with objectives
- Verify the supplier organization and that it can deliver the contracted service
- Verify the roles and responsibilities of transferred staff

Make sure your sub-contractors aren't using you as an advertising opportunity – without your permission – to attract more clients.

Part two: Communication/understanding

- At an early stage obtain board commitment to outsourcing in principle
- Keep trade unions/staff associations informed throughout
- Clearly define outsourcing objectives – cost, flexibility, speed, expertise, innovation, reliability?
- Ensure that the baseline in terms of service quality and cost is understood
- Do not hype-up customer expectations beforehand, although some expectations are inevitable
- Keep customers informed throughout
- Between announcement and implementation, apprise line managers and staff of expectations
- Reassure users by explaining the contract and how it will be managed
- Ensure that end-users understand their obligations and potential business process changes
- Get the successful supplier to present to staff and selected customers as quickly as possible
- Ensure the requirements, deliverables and responsibilities are understood by all
- Keep procedures simple

Outsourcing

Part three: Management

- Agree a schedule for completing a tendering exercise – stick to it
- Executives must recognize the impact and risks of outsourcing
- The customer contract manager must have a good understanding of the current services
- The customer contract manager should be involved in supplier negotiation and selection
- Beware of supplier's underachievement due to lack of business knowledge and resources
- Open-book accounting should be an objective
- Identify the full cost of services *before* they are outsourced
- Outsource areas which are well understood, not ill-defined problem areas
- Make renewal and termination subject to 12 months. notice on either side

Part four: Human resources

- If staff have to transfer, this is a vital part of contract negotiations
- The transfer of staff is key to *your* future service quality – be willing to relinquish talented people
- Work with the supplier to keep transferred staff motivated
- Encourage continuing social contact with transferred staff
- Identify skills and the people who need to be retained – do not rely on chance

Put any 'verbal' agreements into the written contract – it's a smart tactic that makes the supplier think twice.

Part five: Contract content

- You get what you pay for – and you only get what is in the contract
- Make sure the contract is sufficiently flexible to facilitate changes in business practice
- The prime contractor contract should cover everything within the scope of the outsourced work
- Take great care to avoid ambiguity about the scope and expectations of the contract
- Define formal change control mechanisms and include in the contract

More factors to fuel the outsourcing debate

■ Define SLA's and include in the contract (as an appendix)
■ Define a charging scheme and include in the contract – make it flexible and easy to understand
■ Define provision for contract renegotiation and include in the contract
■ Define penalties and include in the contract
■ Include in the contract any verbal assurances received from the supplier
■ Fully define problem escalation procedure for all parties
■ Define disaster/contingency arrangements

Outsourcing's side order – fixed-term contracts

One thing that is being affected by the massive growth in out-sourcing is long-term employ-ment. Although still accounting for a small per centage, fixed-term contracts are inexorably on the rise. A study by UK outplacement consultants Sanders & Sidney among UK employers showed that the trend was particularly prevalent in larger companies in the public sector in the south of the country. Overall, one-in-five jobs now offered by these companies was on a fixed-term basis.

The study, *On the Move – a report on the growing use of fixed-term contracts in the UK*, reported that employ-ers felt that fixed term contracts would increase and so did the job candidates. Many candidates had already been offered fixed-term employment across a range of roles from head of HR to medical officer. Comments the report, 'Although the trend seemed to be irrefutable, it was by no means a popular one with job candidates; the main problem being they made life planning more diffi-cult.' It added, 'Seventy-five per cent of candidates felt fixed-term contracts inhibited making big financial com-mitments and 71 per cent felt they made long-term plan-ning hard. Only 27 per cent believed they would make no significant difference to the way they had to plan their lives.'

Outsourcing

The most telling question, noted Sanders & Sidney, was 'who had the most to gain – employer or employee?' The resounding response was that it was clearly one-way – with 93 per cent of the job candidates interviewed saying the employer had the most to gain: staff could be hired as needed, specialists could be brought in as required and labour costs could be better managed.

Employers, it appears, have been quick to realize that fixed-term contracts stack the odds firmly in their favour, although they said that they did pose the same time-planning difficulties that candidates faced. While most job-seekers thought that taking a fixed-term contract was better than nothing and could lead to a permanent position, employers gave little indication that was the case. Indeed, as the report concluded, 'The survey highlighted a dichotomy. While employees were wishful in their thinking about fixed-term contracts, employers were equally clear about the commercial realities of their labour requirements and the specific place fixed-term contracts had.' The report ended, 'Employees still sought their "ideal" of an ongoing (theoretically secure) contract, despite the likelihood that most fixed-term contracts would not be converted to such. While every employment, to some extent, offers opportunity, the notion of 'serial contracting' might well be more realistic. If employees hold out for the more traditional notion of work, they may not make the most of the new market opportunities.'

Plan your own out-sourcing strategy that meets your unique needs – don't borrow other's ideas.

From the criteria above any management team planning an outsourcing programme can build their own set of checklists and policies that fit their own unique situation. As research for this book has shown, it is not possible to provide a set of generic checklists that users can slavishly follow. In fact most professional outsource consultants and managers who have gone through the process would counsel strongly against that.

So, a word of advice here. Don't borrow someone else's outsourcing guidelines – at least not down to the last letter of the policy or agreement. Develop your own, using the checklists throughout this book, by applying what others have learned, to your own organization's situation and needs.

What about the bad news?

We also need to remember – as referred to earlier – that contracts, however well planned and spelled out at the beginning – don't always pay off. As our research shows, pressure on outsourcers to provide more than they can deliver can create real problems, as can an outsourcer's overenthusiasm in selling more than they can achieve.

A study by the International Facility Management Association (IFMA), headquartered in Houston, Texas, has shown that companies are recording disappointments with outsourcing, most of which back up the warning signals that I have already set out in this book. But, again, before getting into outsourcing programmes, look at areas where others have failed and consider these when you are negotiating contracts with outside vendors (Table 5.1).

Don't wait too long in your evaluation procedure. If it is going badly, be ready to get out and bring it back in-house.

Table 5.1 Disadvantages for outsourcing/out-tasking

Contract employees less company oriented	51%
Lengthy bid process	44%
Longer response time to problems	35%
Loss of control	31%
Poor-quality workers	29%
Difficult to change vendors	25%
Reduced quality	24%
Time-consuming to supervise contract	23%
Low level of service	23%
Increased turnover	22%
Increased costs	18%
Burden on purchasing	12%
No disadvantages	9%

Source: Outsourcing, International Facility Management Association 1993

In addition, the IFMA research showed that a quarter of the companies they surveyed for their study had in fact brought services back in-house for quality improvement (Table 5.2).

Outsourcing

Table 5.2 Why services were brought back in-house after being outsourced (includes only respondents who had brought back services in-house)

To better control quality	66%
To reduce costs	54%
To regain control	50%
To improve quality	50%
To improve response time	45%
Dissatisfaction with provider	35%
No longer needed	12%
To reduce turnover and training costs	7%
Service no longer available	2%

Source: Outsourcing, International Facility Management Association, 1993

While neither of these findings show that outsourcing programmes are disasters waiting to happen, they do underline that it is necessary to be cautious about who you deal with, and that it is not possible to think you have washed your hands of a problem just because you have contracted it out.

Ten pieces of advice from Texaco

Texaco's Corporate Service Department has a record for careful outsourcing programmes. Here Corporate Services manager, Colin Bannerman, gives ten points of advice to remember for would-be outsourcers:

- **Any area or activity can be outsourced. However, the company should have a *clear* direction and strategy to follow before committing to move functions outside its direct control.**
- **The most successful outsourcing projects have moved indirect functions for the host company to an outsourced supplier whose *main* business it is.**
- ***Warning!* If the vendor is using the services he is providing you as an add-on to attract clients, there will be little focus on the success of the new structure.**
- **One of the largest *barriers* is the cultural acceptance of**

a supplier relationship, rather than an internal service, largely because the hierarchy and power-base of many managers is built on direct control or position authority. The conflict between these dimensions creates instability with external providers – recognition and reward systems must be retuned to support new management practices.

■ Good communications and shared values both formally in a contract and informally in the culture of the two organizations are important. If services or quality are important a method of managing through the contractor must be found.

■ A measurement system should be used to determine direction and success for the outsourcing programme. However, *there are no universal measures* with which to grade all services.

■ Don't follow the US examples just because they exist. Any outsourcing must be justified as a good course of action in your own situation each and every time.

■ The drivers for sourcing/outsourcing come from technological change and resource management. If these factors evolve differently due to *location* and/or *timing* then the sourcing questions should be answered differently.

■ Consultants are valuable in breaking the mind-set of managers and companies. However, changes introduced by consultants will not change companies unless the managers and employees work with the new system.

■ If companies find that advantage can be gained by bringing services under direct management why not? The drivers for *in* or *out* sourcing, should be considered – *not* the fashion.

Watch out for selective outsourcing

One area that outsource enthusiasts need to be very careful with is selective outsourcing – having a host of sub-contractors, supposedly interlinking with each other but being managed by the outsourcer. Reported experience again shows that in many cases single suppliers managed their own little portion of the process very well, but were either

Outsourcing

unwilling or incapable of interacting with others. Because of this, managers in the sourcing company find themselves spending an increased, rather than a reduced, amount of time coordinating the process, arbitrating in sub-contractor disputes and demarcation lines of where one stops and the other begins.

But the other side is that if you rely on one, major provider, say for all your FM or all your IT, you have the opposite: not enough management control and your hands severely tied. As I said earlier, you have to choose what is right for your organization, not base your decisions and actions on the experiences of others.

Another point to keep in mind is that any successful outsourcing contract has to be a dynamic document that takes into account changing business conditions. If we are all managing in a world of constant change and ambiguity, having a contract that is set in concrete isn't going to do much even in the short term, never mind a longer period.

Fari Akhlaghi, head of the Unit for Facilities Management Research at Sheffield Hallam University agrees, saying that 'a service contract needs to be a living document. That is to say that in addition to fulfilling its role in protecting the rights and interests of the parties involved, which is a legal issue, it has to be a useful framework and the symbol for a strong partnership between service purchaser and service provider.' According to Akhlaghi's view, 'Such a contract, in addition to its pure legal parts, such as indemnities, will have a "live" engine made up of three key components (Figure 5.1):

- Statements of desired service outcomes in both threshold and incremental value terms, expressed in hard and soft measures
- A service improvement and cost reduction mechanism – a moving specification
- Measurement and review procedures using the same values and measurements expressed in the components above.

Appoint an experienced executive to manage the process – friendly, experienced, but tough-minded are good traits to go for.

Don't let your outsourcing contract set in concrete. Like other aspects of your business, change is going to drive how your relationship develops

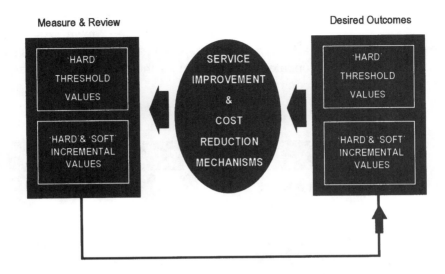

Figure 5.1 The basic structure of a living FM contract

What gives the contract its life is the component called the moving specification. While Akhlaghi ruefully notes that 'the very notion of anything moving in a legal contract is not something that the lawyers would normally find agreeable, it is essential that the moving specification should form part of the body of the contract and change over time with the agreement of the parties involved.' Interestingly, Akhlaghi's ideas are in line with the findings of the Outsourcing Institute in this chapter, whose own research shows that contracts must be agreed and managed by business managers not the legal profession.

Akhlaghi has developed a format for this moving specification, which can be adapted by any organization to make a workable model of an outsourcing process. Figure 5.2 shows the format of a typical moving specification.

For illustrative purposes, in the case illustrated in Figure 5.2 (which is based on patient catering in a hospital), five quality performance areas have been identified for the service against each of these five items and certain key parameters are formally recorded. The current status is recorded in the first column, followed by the minimum and future quality targets. The time by which these quality targets are to be achieved is then recorded and next to it the improvement task will be carried out. The financial implications of the actions are recorded in the next column. Finally, it is important that the risks of not achieving the targets are agreed, identified and written down. As targets are achieved, new targets will replace them and this situation is updated with respect to the financial performance of the contract.

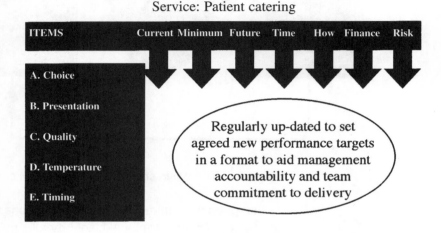

Service: Patient catering

Figure 5.2 A moving specification for outsourcing. (*Source*: Fari Akhlaghi, Unit for Facilities Management Research, Sheffield Hallam University)

Get yourself a contract manager

Most experienced outsourcers say that one thing that can really help the outsourcing process, especially in developing relationships, is to appoint a contract manager or relationship manager who has the responsibility of making it all work. Successful outsourcers suggest tha what you need for this role is a manager with an outgoing personality, who gets on well with people, but also knows both the overall business the company is in as well as a thorough knowledge of the area that is to be outsourced to a sub-contractor. You also have to be sure that they are 'tough' enough to demand and get full

More factors to fuel the outsourcing debate

explanations when and where problems arise and have the 'business courage' to recommend termination of a contract if it is not in the best or long-term interests of the company.

Fari Akhlaghi further explains this moving specification model. 'As we would be operating on a financially incentive-based contract, in the early part of most contracts based on the above system, the quality targets will need to be achieved and costs of operation reduced at the same time. There comes a point, however, when any increases in productivity levels and cost reductions will result in unacceptable reductions in quality; or when improvements in quality and service cannot be sustained with existing levels of costs. These points will be arrived at differently in different contracts. So the final solution in each case will have to be a modification of the remuneration package, which can largely be planned into the contract from the outset.'

Akhlaghi firmly believes that contracts of this type will become a regular part of the outsourcing process. As he says, 'there is every indication in the market that suppliers of FM services are willing to enter into these new generation of contracts. For some of them, such opportunities provide a strong vehicle to differentiate themselves in the market as "value" and "service" oriented contractors, as distinct from "cost-based" suppliers of "commodity" and standardized services against tight specifications.'

His view is backed up by Charles Cox, group sales and marketing director at UK-based FM providers Hoskyns. Writing in the *Financial Times*, he noted an already changed climate in the outsourcer's expectations. 'The key to change, however, lies in the behaviour of the buyer,' he noted. 'Leading customers are no longer buying a facilities management service as if it were a commodity, and their understanding of how to gain the best value for their business is evolving. Customers are becoming choosier about the form of service they buy, how they buy it and, more importantly, what they do with it.'

Outsourcing – especially in the FM – arena is a rapidly evolving process. While nothing is better than practical experience, a lot of the views and ideas presented here can give most companies a headstart into building their own successful outsourcing programmes. But before all of us go rushing off to get started, let's consider the human element in all this.

Think about your people

International management consultant and human resources expert Mark Thomas, author of the influential book *Supercharge Your Management Role*, says that any manager considering outsourcing has to make sure that he or she take the people in the business along and ensure they know where they are going. 'They haven't signed up for a mystery tour' says Thomas.

Thomas offers some very useful guidelines of what and what not to do when people come into the outsourcing equation:

1 Think about the background to the deal or outsourcing. Has it been friendly, aggressive, hostile or collaborative? – as this will determine the likely people reactions following the event.
2 Remember that people may have
   ■ Fear of the unknown
   ■ Anxiety over the future
   ■ Uncertainty over the future
   ■ Nostalgia for the old days
   ■ Hostility to the new (frequently)
   ■ Resistance to the new name, structure, operations
   ■ Resentment over loss of identity
   All these factors will need to be managed in advance of any outsourcing so you need to major in on the communications side:
   ■ People will want to hear what is going on from top management
   ■ Avoid any communications vacuum. Better to say you don't know than nothing as that only creates further tensions
3 Remember, people will be reading everything into management's actions so:
   ■ Be clear on the timescales for the transition
   ■ Explain how peoples' employment rights and

conditions will be impacted in the light of employment legislation

■ Involve if possible any new owners in early presentations and allow them to explain their plans
■ Create a positive atmosphere but at the same time recognize that some people will be grieving
■ Throw a party to celebrate – provide an opportunity for people to let off steam about the change!

4 New owners should move fast. Don't delay any bad news – people expect change. Simply waiting two months for things to settle and then moving bad news is no good. People expect change, so better to strike as soon as possible.

5 Focus on the positives but be clear as to the challenges that the organization must face

Checklist for people on the end of the change

■ Think about the bad aspects of the old set-up as well as the good
■ Recognize that the changes may well bring new opportunities – more effective ways of operating, less control, more freedom
■ Start thinking about a contingency plan. 'What if I do not like the set-up?' Be clear as to your options under the changes
■ Discuss the future with the old and new management. Be clear as to what options you have
■ Get your CV up to date
■ Review your network of contacts. Start to warm them up in the event that you do not like the changes
■ Meet new owners with a positive outlook. They are no doubt looking to make the thing a success so reflect their optimism
■ Avoid negative and critical comments – you don't want to be highlighted as a 'blocker' or 'cynic'
■ Remember, the event is going to happen regardless of your feelings or views and if you don't like the changes then simply be positive and use the time to find another career opening. Incurring the criticism of any new owners is likely to see you marked as someone who

Outsourcing

does not feature in any future plans. Far better to leave on your terms and in your time than anyone else's
■ **Think about other opportunities. Is it a good time to make a change?**

Don't forget the human element

There are a lot of stories and examples around of companies who did throw the baby out with the bath water. Desperate to create more capacity they took either new ideas and outsourced their production – losing, or never ever getting the manufacturing skills they may need along the line – or existing production outside to make room for new products – and promptly forgot how to make the old, often successful lines.

Frequently, failure to develop proper partnership ties with the sub-contractor have resulted in all kinds of acrimony, legal battles and, worse still, lost profits. And while much of that has gone on in manufacturing industry – where there was perhaps a need to quickly move on a breakthrough idea and get it to market fast -, we are now seeing the same sort of effect beginning to take place in services.

Despite the rise and rise of IT as a dominant part of all our businesses, when it comes to service-related industry, there is one other key commodity – people. People have the ideas, people interact with the customers, people program and press computer keys. There is a major downside to all this – people are expensive, especially when they have been around for a long time and have, as one outplacement consultant said – 'unfortunate delusions of entitlement.'

So far there hasn't been a great deal of bleating from service industry employees – who have, on the whole, been more likely to change jobs in a more flexible and fluid industry than that of manufacturing – but employers bent on outsourcing as a long-term strategy had better think long and hard of the human consequences of their actions. History shows that it is all too easy to give people things, but it is a lot harder to take them away. Witness the problems countries like Germany, France and Belgium are having in trying to cut social benefits; look what major US employers like GM and Boeing are going through in trying to get a more flexible manufacturing approach – the unions don't like it and they will probably continue not to like it.

More factors to fuel the outsourcing debate

Whatever you do, don't forget your people. Keep them informed and don't let rumours start.

In the service business with its history of less unionization, a lot of part-time and fixed-contract work, making changes to the workforce is a lot less traumatic – at least it has been until now.

But employers embarking on outsourcing need to consider carefully some of the things that they may be letting themselves in for if they begin the process and what it could mean in a negative way for their businesses. Loss of talent and expertise inside the organization is only one element of the impact a poorly planned outsourcing programme can have. Complications with employees' rights and entitlements, unfair dismissals and wrangling with new vendors can all contribute to wasting much of the management time you thought you had freed up. My suggestion is that anyone embarking on an outsourcing process where people will be transferred or find their roles changing should use the checklist outlined above, and as KPMG/Impact programme says, 'stick to it'.

Many commentators credit the US bounce-back from recession and the creation of millions of new jobs as a false picture, stating that those new jobs are not permanent – if ever there was such a thing in the USA – but semi-permanent, lower skilled and often part-time. Critics have written about 'a nation of hamburger flippers' and certainly statistics show that real earnings in the USA have not risen – only wives going out to work have kept US families ahead of the 1960s real wage levels. In Europe downsizing and rightsizing has taken its toll in a different way, creating a mass of solid, immovable, unsolvable unemployment, that averages around 11 per cent of the workforce and gets as high as 25 per cent in countries like Spain. The problem in Europe is exactly the opposite of the problem in the USA.

In the USA workers are taken on and shed like leaves on a tree, in Europe no-one is hiring. They are finding other ways with technology, with overseas outsourcing, with – to be frank – illegal hiring policies to get around a system that makes it just too costly to hire. Into the midst of those two opposite ways of looking at and dealing with the workforce comes outsourcing – a new phenomenon, that if we are to accept it as not just a short-term cost cutter but a long-term strategic policy is going to have far-reaching consequences for all of us, employer and employee alike.

Outsourcing

Think about it this way. In the USA the CEO of the ABC Corporation signs an outsourcing agreement with the XYZ Corporation. It stipulates that they take on board the responsibility for 150 ABC employees – guaranteeing them full rights. Those rights are a six-month ceiling on unemployment compensation, which doesn't amount to very much and is certainly worth the outsourcer's investment.

In Europe the managing director of a similar ABC Company signs an outsourcing agreement within the XYZ Corporation, with the same terms and conditions. The XYZ Corporation may think twice or even three times about it as the employees may well have 12, 24 or even 48 months of compensation riding on their heads, not to mention massive social security payments to their governments and high pension entitlements.

Where employees are included in the move they are rarely offered alternatives, such as voluntary redundancy. What this means is that if the job they were doing at ABC is 'sold' to the XYZ vendor, then they have to go along with it – even if it is in another location, although some national legislation may rule against this after a long wrangle in the courts. Interestingly enough, relocation has already been used by several French and German corporations to get people to jump ship of their own volition, thereby negating their employee compensation rights. One French giant moved from Paris to a rural location 200 kilometres away. The resulting 'voluntary' shakeout lowered the average age by seven years. So much lower are overall US wage levels and their attendant low social security that vendor companies are offering a goodwill package of a guaranteed one year of working when ABC's employees arrive to work at XYZ. In parts of Europe that could be financial suicide.

Comments Kevan Wooden, European controller of the facility management group Procord, 'In mainland Europe outsourcing is considerably behind and this has much to do with government policy. The UK policies that have made it so attractive to outside investors (currently receiving 40 per cent of all inward investment to Europe) have helped outsourcing companies. Anti-union legislation, more relaxed labour laws and lower benefit scales make it easier to transfer employees to an outsourcer in the UK than in the rest of Europe – where equal rights directives and the inability to make restructuring decisions often hamper cost-reduction exercises.'

More factors to fuel the outsourcing debate

The Outsourcing Institute's Michael Corbett concurs, pointing out that the drive to seek out and outsource to the best in the business, wherever they are, could be affected. 'The differences will be where there are legal or cultural restrictions on implementing these types of organizational change and the pursuit of 'best-in-world' providers, wherever they are. For example, some mainland European countries are effectively "unionized" by law, which will slow the process, just as it has in unionized companies in the USA.'

Far likelier in mainland Europe is a trend to create start-ups with small staffs that can take the tax breaks offered new companies and let the old company languish or even go bankrupt. Another trend is to spin off high-performing divisions and set them up as wholly separate outsourced divisions.

The big outsourcing operators are reacting cautiously to the situation, not wanting to be labelled angels of death. Their argument is that with their areas of operations expanding they are always looking for new staff and therefore the problem is irrelevant. The fact is that it is not irrelevant, far from it. Certainly some may get career-enhancing positions – if they are prepared to relocate – but for others it is not a happy experience (Figure 5.3).

IT and FM staff are being transferred like soccer players from one company to another, expected to change locations with little warning and no special compensation or any incentives for agreeing to the transfer. These are not high flyers who plan it that way, these are average Joe's and Janes, who are in work because they have to earn a living. Companies owe it to their staffs to consider what it will do to these people and how it will affect their lives, well before they start the outsourcing process.

The other danger for individuals – and low-skill, low-pay individuals at that – is that much of the facilities management area is in either short-term contract hire or part-time employment. Consequently, many of the people doing this work can be fairly transient, their skill level is doubtful and their loyalty questionable.

What management who are planning to use outsourced FM services need to ask themselves is whether this meets their needs. As we have seen elsewhere in this book, one of the biggest criticisms of outsourcing has been by managers who asked firms to do work they were patently not qualified to carry out. With low-skill people and part-time workers, managers need to stipulate exactly what they are going to get.

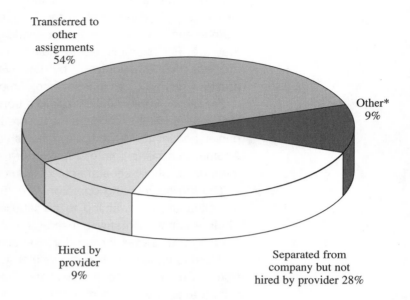

Transferred to
other
assignments
54%

Other*
9%

Hired by
provider
9%

Separated from
company but not
hired by provider 28%

Figure 5.3 The consequences for displaced employees (based on employers with outsourcing experience or plans citing actions taken for the majority of employees). *Respondents unable to specify action taken for most employees because of multiple outsourcing initiatives. (*Source*: *Outsourcing HR Services*, The Conference Board, 1994)

What employers are faced with is a dichotomy. Failure to innovate and keep up with others who can could spell disaster. Going ahead without the right considerations can bring a lot of surprises that few have planned in advance. This means that is really is necessary to consider your workforce – all of it, not just those about to change firms. Communicate, communicate, communicate may sound like back-to-basics advice, but it does work and it is often overlooked.

This type of change creates rumours, tensions and destroys motivation and productivity. Careful planning, careful thinking and clear, unambiguous communications and counselling with all those involved can make the process worthwhile for everyone.

More factors to fuel the outsourcing debate

Change is all around us, and our people need to change as much as we do. Unfortunately they are often less well-equipped to handle new working arrangements. If we do embrace outsourcing we must be able to explain why we are doing it, what advantages it will bring and what it will mean to them. You might know the reasons only too well, don't expect them to see it or understand it the same way.

Careful thought and a lot of tender loving communication are going to help a great deal. Plan it and stick to it!

Executive summary

- *Warning!* make sure your sub-contractors aren't using you to attract more clients.

- Don't follow the example of others just because one way worked for them. Plan your own outsourcing strategy that meets your unique needs.

- Appoint an experienced executive to manage the process – friendly, experienced and tough are good traits.

- Don't let the finance and legal considerations run your outsourcing negotiations – it's about doing business and building trust.

- Don't get bullied by the vendor, it's your business not theirs.

- Don't play favourites, no matter how compelling the reason. Only ask for tenders from companies you have pre-qualified.

- Don't oversell what service or savings you are going to get – you may be disappointed.

- Put any 'verbal' agreements into the written contract.

- If it is going badly, be ready to get out and bring it back in-house.

Outsourcing

- As we all learn more about how outsourcing contracts are changing, don't get yours set in stone.

- Whatever you do, don't forget your people. Keep them informed and don't let rumours start.

6

The road ahead

At the beginning of this book there are statistics about the expected growth of outsourcing to the year 2000, billions and billions of dollars, deutschemarks, pounds and francs are going to thrown into this ever expanding pot. In fact although many of these forecasts are by sane, intelligent individuals and organizations, they are most likely wrong. They will – as with predictions about IT – underestimate what history will ultimately reveal. No-one can really say what the effect the outsourcing phenomenon will have on our economies, our organizations – even ourselves. But one thing is clear, it is going to take off in an unprecedented way. Competitive pressures are going to force organizations in even the most controlled nations to look at other options – or they will most likely perish. Whether this will mean that short-sighted politicians will do anything to help remains to be seen. Most likely they will have little choice as businesses will simply relocate to more favourable, competitive climates.

The inability of an organization to know everything will mean that alliances and partnerships – already major global forces – will have to increase. How long they remain twinned, or even stay friends, is open to question, speculation and a great deal of debate.

Technology, and its gift for allowing us to do business around the world, across borders instantaneously, is going to be the major driver of outsourcing, or sourcing, growth. Those with access and the ability to fully embrace what technology can do will be the winners.

Above all, and what this book has clearly illustrated, is that outsourcing is not a single phenomenon and it is not just a current fad. Indeed, as the experts who contributed to this

Outsourcing

book have emphasized time and time again, it is what *you* and *your* organization make it.

What has been the most fundamental discovery in researching and writing this book is that outsourcing is two things:

- It can be a tactical, short-term attempt to solve some already serious problems. Managed right, it can have – has had – some great successes.
- It is increasingly being seen – and championed – as much more than a tactical weapon. It can be – and has proven to be – a strategic weapon, that is not a one-time, singular event or idea but a total process that if adopted correctly, transcends divisions, departments and disciplines.

That, I think, is the most important lesson that this book can teach. That outsourcing is a phenomenon that can become a key strategic part of driving companies forward. Management experts today talk not of following a strategic direction but of navigating the enterprise towards its future. They explain that with so much change and ambiguity, choosing a direction is irrelevant and most likely to be the wrong destination: for, by the time you get there, your true goal will be different. What they advocate is being equipped with the right organization – the right ship – to constantly change direction as the winds and currents of the global economy shift.

Outsourcing is one of the most powerful tools that any captain of industry can have aboard the organizational ship. It has unlimited use and covers whatever business you want to be in and whatever business you want to be out of.

That, of course, brings us to the key point. Outsourcing makes good strategic sense when you know what you are going to outsource and why. As that great man of management Peter Drucker once said in an interview, 'management by objectives makes a great deal of sense if you know what your objectives are – nine times out of ten you don't.' That same warning can apply to outsourcing.

All the experts counsel us to 'hold on to our core businesses'. That's OK as long as we have taken the time and put the energy into knowing just what they are. We know there are stories about corporations outsourcing business areas that appeared to be less than strategic, only to realize their mistakes at a later date. Similarly, there are frightening war stories, of organizations that have got into less than friendly alliances and joint ventures – losing their competitive edge in the process.

in brief

'Very few functions will be judged to be core to an organization.' – *New Directions in Finance*, Economist Intelligence Unit, 1995

Looking to the future, we have all heard predictions of the virtual corporation that consists of loosely networked specialists – the ultimate outsourced organization – with only the slender thread of the Internet to hold it in place. Others call this direction that the totally outsourced organization could take the 'hollow corporation'. That description may well be apt. If there is nothing there, then where are all the ideas, the motivation, the loyalties, the excitement of interaction?

During the research for this book I was very impressed by a reference to an article by Robert Vrancken, a facilities planner and designer in the USA who made a great deal of sense, and not only summed up how we should think about outsourcing in a practical way, but suggested we look beyond as well. This is what he said. 'When considering the outsourcing process as an alternative, it's important to remember that one size does not fit all. Whether the functions are eventually outsourced or insourced, the associated costs, expected performance levels, cultural implications and management requirements are not the same in all organizations, or even within an industry.' This, however is Robert Vrancken's telling point. 'There is an additional, but often overlooked, consideration. Many times the needed expertise is in fact "under foot" – it just requires the proper guidance and management.'

So, if you are going to embark on an outsourcing programme take care. In fact take great care. Take the advice of the experts in this book. Their collected wisdom can save you and your colleagues a great deal of time, energy and

Outsourcing

expense, but don't forget that the best solution is not always the new one, or the most visible – you might have it already.

Throughout the book I have assembled short, concise pieces of advice, ideas that can help you understand and use the outsourcing process. To make it easier to use, or review that advice – all based on the input of the experts quoted throughout the book – I have listed them all below. Although in no particular order of importance, they do add to the usefulness of this 'How To' guide and are worth sharing with your colleagues when you consider outsourcing options. At the end there is space to add issues, ideas and actions that are unique to your own business.

- ■ It helps to make sure that whoever you are dealing with in the outsourcing business understands clearly your definitions otherwise major confusion can arise. It may sound simple – *it's not*!
- ■ Business life today is just too complicated to do everything in-house. Everyone outsources something – think about it!
- ■ Outsourcing isn't new, it's just the emphasis on it that's changed how we think about it.
- ■ Outsourcing can be a two-way street. You can outsource your non-core business and insource from others who can't match your capabilities.
- ■ Outsourcing is being seen less and less as a tactical, cost-saving drive and more and more as a strategic direction that the organization follows.
- ■ Don't confuse outsourcing with cost-cutting. Chances are it won't work for long and you'll lose out big!
- ■ Never sign an outsourcing agreement without considering carefully the longer-term implications – too many have, to their regret.
- ■ Control, control, control – that's a central outsourcing issue that too many forget.
- ■ Don't sign up with a consultant who treats outsourcing as the flavour of the month. Look for a specialist firm that has experience.
- ■ Organizations are still using short-term outsourcing techniques as knee-jerk, 'we're in trouble' cost-cutting exercises. If you are doing that make sure you know why.
- ■ Never outsource what you don't understand. Outsource things you *can* do, but would rather not – that way you keep control.

The road ahead

- There are now clearly two levels of outsourcing – tactical (short-term, results-driven) and strategic (long-term, process-driven). Make sure you know which you are doing.
- While it is easier to start from scratch, you can change your culture if you know why you are doing it and know what you want.
- Outsourcing gives managers time to concentrate on the things they do well – don't confuse it with getting rid of the things you don't like.
- As organizations become more process driven, outsourcing is a natural fit with new business structures and it forces businesses to define their core competencies.
- Outsourcing isn't about cost savings, it's about more effective performance in the longer-term.
- Successful outsourcing organizations do a great deal more than what is called for in the 'letter' of the relationship, they really build partnerships.
- Don't think traditional. Think about what you'd like to be as an organization, then try to achieve it. It takes belief in yourselves that you can make it work
- Define your outsourcing requirements in clear, complete and measurable terms and stick with them – you'll be glad you did.
- Look for outsourcers with whom you have a cultural fit – who regard their business the way you do.
- An outsourcing relationship is most often based on reputation, references and existing contacts – think of who you already know before you waste lots of time.
- Use outsourcing as a way to get back to basics and improve your business focus – it can be the clean sheet of white paper that all our organizations need from time to time.
- Giving people the ownership of your problems makes them your partner, but remember it isn't just a cheap way of doing business. You want the vendor to succeed as well.
- Linked solely to short-term concerns, companies are often disappointed with the results that outsourcing brings. If your ambition is to cut costs, don't expect too much.
- The idea of outsourcing scares people too! Communicate, communicate, communicate. Take them

Outsourcing

along with you – don't leave them wallowing behind in a sea of uncertainty.

■ World-class business service providers are beginning to offer regional and global solutions as opposed to local or national. If you're in that league, it may be the way to go – very soon.

■ Remember the purchasing department? Suddenly it's important. But do they know enough to meet today's mixed bag of outsourcing requirements?

■ External FM outsourcing is really doing excellently what companies have done poorly – or ignored completely – themselves. There's nothing clever about it, just a new focus on something you dismissed as unimportant.

■ Be careful what you buy, how you buy it and who you buy it from – quick decisions don't pay off!

■ In the coming years, the FM market is going to get tougher, with more competitors and more choice. Make sure you can take advantage of those changes – don't get locked into long-term, inflexible agreements.

■ Make sure your sub-contractors aren't using you as an advertising opportunity – without your permission – to attract more clients.

■ Plan your own outsourcing strategy that meets your unique needs – don't borrow others ideas.

■ Appoint an experienced executive to manage the process – friendly, experienced, but tough-minded are good traits to go for.

■ Don't let the finance or legal function run your outsourcing negotiations – it's about doing business and building trust, use managers who want to do business, not write contracts.

■ Remember, it's *your* business. Don't get bullied into agreeing things you don't want or don't need.

■ Don't play favourites, no matter how compelling the reason. Only ask for tenders from companies you have pre-qualified and stick to that strategy.

■ Don't oversell your management on what great service or savings you are going to get – you may be disappointed, especially in the short term.

■ Put any 'verbal' agreements into the written contract – it's a smart tactic that makes the supplier think twice.

chapter 6

The road ahead

■ Don't wait to long in your evaluation procedure. If it is going badly, be ready to get out and bring it back in-house.

■ Don't get your outsourcing contract set in stone. Like other aspects of your business, change is going to drive how your relationship develops.

■ Whatever you do, don't forget your people. Keep them informed and don't let rumours start.

Whether you totally embrace the concept of outsourcing as a major strategic process that can advance the way you think and develop your business, or you see it as a tactical tool to be used as and when required, take the advice that is on offer here. You and your colleagues will be very glad you did.

Outsourcing resource list

3I Group plc
91 Waterloo Road
London SE1 8XP
UK
Tel: +44 171 928 3131
Fax: + 44 171 928 0058
*UK Survey No. 12: *Outsourcing*

Fari Akhlaghi
Head of Unit for Facilties Management Research
School of Urban and Regional Studies
Sheffield Hallam Univeristy
City Campus
Sheffield S1 1WB
UK
Tel: +44 114 253 3240
Fax: +44 114 253 4038
E-mail: UFMR@SHU.AC.UK

Andersen Consulting
2 Arundel Street
London WC2R 3LT
UK
Tel: +44 171 438 5000
Fax: +44 171 831 1133
WWW: http://www.ac.com
*Harris UK Outsourcing Study, 'Independent research reveals unexpected benefits of outsourcing'
*Intersect: *A Study on Outsourcing*, 1993
*Executive Briefing, *New Directions in Finance*, with The Economist Intelligence Unit

Outsourcing

Colin Bannerman
Manager Corporate Services
Texaco Ltd
Corporate Services Department
1 Westferry Circus
Canary Wharf
London E14 4HA
UK
Tel: +44 171 719 3000
Fax: +44 171 719 5130

Lawrence Beuttner
First Chicago
525 West Monroe Street
Mail Suite 0295
Chicago
Illinois 60661
USA
Tel: +1 312 441 4001
Fax: +1 312 441 4099

The Business Round Table Ltd
18 Devonshire Street
London W1N 1FS
UK
Tel: +44 171 363 6951
Fax: +44 171 636 6952
Thinking About Facilities Management

Centre for Facilities Management
Strathclyde Graduate Business School
199 Cathedral Street
Glasgow G4 0QU
UK
Tel: +44 141 553 4165
Fax: +44 141 552 7299
An Overview of the Facilities Management Industry 1995,
Parts I, II ,III

Chi-Chi's International (CCI)
Steenweg op Brussel, 541 – Box 1
B-3090 Overijse
Belgium
Tel: +32 2 657 05 55

Outsourcing resource list

Fax: +32 2 657 02 47
E-mail: 100121.204@compuserve.com

The Conference Board Europe
Chaussée de La Hulpe 130, Box 11
B-1000 Brussels
Belgium
Tel: +32 2 675 54 05
Fax: +32 2 675 03 95

Paul Cooper
E-mail: 100600.1430@compuserve.com

Michael Corbett & Associates Ltd
3 Neptune Road
Suite A-28
Poughkeepsie
NY 12601
USA
Tel: +1 914 463 1110
Fax: + 1 914 463 1534
E-mail: mfcorbett@Corbett Associates.com

Deloitte & Touche Consulting Group
Suite 900
600 Renaissance Center
Detroit, MI 48243-1704
USA
Tel: +1 313 396 3032
Fax: +1 313 396 3400
E-mail: kmamola@dttus.com
WWW: http://www.dttus.com/hometext.htm

DHL Intern srl
Vle Milanofiori
Strada 5 Pal. U/3
I-20090 Assago (Mi)
Italy
Tel: + 39 2 575721
Fax: +39 2 89208114

Lisa Ellram
Department of Business Administration
Arizona State College of Business
Arizona State University

Outsourcing

Tempe, AZ 85287-3706
USA
Tel: + 1 602 965 55 16

Exel Logistics
Merton Centre
45 St. Peter's Street
Bedford MK40 2UB
UK
Tel: +44 1234 273727

Expatriate Management Ltd (EML)
Paxton House
26-30 Artillery Lane
London E1 7LS
UK
Tel: +44 171 247 2299
Fax: +44 171 392 7000
E-mail: 106030.400@compuserve.com

Facilities Management Association
ESCA House
34 Palace Court
Bayswater
London W2 4JG
UK
Tel: +44 171 727 5238
Fax: +44 171 727 5238

Gail Hartley
Business Support Unit
Mowlem Facilities Management
Hetton Court
The Oval
Hunslet
Leeds LS10 2AU
UK
Tel: +44 113 270 5533
Fax: +44 113 270 1133
E-mail: sales@trilogy.co.uk

HMSO
St Crispins
Duke Street
Norwich NR3 1PD

Outsourcing resource list

UK
Tel: +44 1603 622211
Fax: +44 1603 696784
E-mail: suzanne.kerby@hmso.gov.uk

Hooker Cockram Ltd.
32-34 Burwood Road
Hawthorn
Victoria 3122
Australia
Tel: +61 3 9819 5182
Fax: +61 3 9818 7734
E-mail: email@hcl.com.au

IBM Global Network
PO Box 30021
Tampa, FL 33630
USA
Tel: +1 800 775 5808

IBM United Kingdom Ltd.
South Bank
76 Upper Ground
London SE1 9PZ
UK
Tel:+ 44 171 202 5612

International Data Corporation (IDC)
2 Bath Road
Chiswick
London W4 1LN
UK
Tel: +44 181 995 8082
Fax: +44 181 747 0212
*Business Strategies for Outsourcing

International Facility Management Association (IFMA)
1 East Greenway Plaza
11th Floor
Houston, Texas 77046-0194
USA
Tel: +1 623 4362
Fax: +1 713 623 6124
E-mail: webmaster@ifma.org
*Research Report #10: Outsourcing

Outsourcing

International Facility Management Association (IFMA)
European Bureau
Boulevard At-Michel 15
B-1040 Brussels
Belgium
Tel: +32 2 743 15 42
Fax: +32 2 743 15 50
E-mail: 100332.670@compuserve.com

ISS Europe
1 Meyskensstraat 224
B-1780 Wemmel
Belgium
Tel: +32 2 456 05 60
Fax: + 32 2 456 05 89
E-mail: FNURSKI@pophost.eunet.be
WWW: http://www.iss.dk

KPMG Impact Programme
8 Salisbury Square
London EC4Y 8BB
UK
Tel: +44 171 311 1000
Fax: +44 171 311 3993
WWW: http://www.KPMG.com
Outsourcing, Best Practice Guidelines

Sandra Lester
The Conference Board Europe
Chaussée de La Hulpe 130, Box 11
B-1000 Brussels
Belgium
Tel: +32 2 675 54 05
Fax: +32 2 675 03 95

Scott Lever
Department of Management
IU School of Business
Tenth and Fee Lane
Bloomington, IN 47405
USA
Tel: +1 812 855 9200
Fax: +1 812 855 8679

Outsourcing resource list

E-mail: SLever@Indiana.edu
An Analysis of Managerial Motivations Behind Outsourcing Practices in Human Resources

K. Alexander
Centre for Facilities Management
Strathclyde Graduate Business School
199 Cathedral Street
Glasgow G4 0QU
UK
Tel: +44 141 553 4165
Fax: +44 141 552 7299
E-mail: Alexander@SGBS.Strath.ac.uk

Management Support Technology (MST)
E-mail: mst@mstnet.com
*'IT outsourcing: operational improvement or strategic imperative', An MST Working Paper on outsourcing strategies

Anthony Miller
International Data Corporation (IDC)
2 Bath Road
Chiswick
London W4 1LN
UK
Tel: +44 181 995 8082
Fax: +44 181 747 0212
E-mail: A.MILLER@IDG.GEIS.COM

Bob Milne
Hooker Cockram Ltd.
32-34 Burwood Road
Hawthorn
Victoria 3122
Australia
Tel: +61 3 9819 5182
Fax: +61 3 9818 7734
E-mail: robmil@hcl.com.au

Jerry Mirelli
Executive VP
TBI
50 Tice Boulevard

Outsourcing

Woodcliff Lake NJ 08852
USA
Tel: +1 201 573 0400
Fax: +1 201 573 9191
E-mail: jmirelli@tbi.mhs.compuserve.com

Mowlem Facilities Management
Hetton Court
The Oval
Hunslet
Leeds LS10 2AU
UK
Tel: +44 113 270 5533
Fax: +44 113 270 1133
E-mail: sales@trilogy.co.uk

The Outsourcing Institute
45 Rockefeller Plaza
Suite 2000
New York, NY 10111
USA
Tel: +1 800 421 6767
Fax: =1 800 421 1644
E-mail: MCORBETT@outsourcing.com
WWW: http://www.outsourcing.com
Purchasing Dynamics, Expectations and Outcomes, An Outsourcing Instate Trends Report – 1995

PA Consulting Group
123 Buckingham Palace Road
London SW1W 9SR
UK
Tel: +44 171 730 9000
Fax: +44 171 333 5050
Management Summary: International Strategic Sourcing Survey 1996

Penton Research Services
1100 Superior Avenue
Cleveland
Ohio 44114-2543
USA
Tel: +1 800 736 8660
Fax: +1 216 696 8130

Outsourcing resource list

E-mail: pentonrsch@aol.com
WWW: http://www.penton.com/corp/research

Procord
2 The Briars
Waterberry Drive
Waterlooville
Hampshire PO7 7YH
UK
Tel: +44 1705 230 500
Fax: +44 1705 230 501

Pye Tait Associates
5 Royal Parade
Harrogate
North Yorkshire HG1 2SZ
UK
Tel: +44 1423 509433
Fax: +44 1423 509502
E-mail: 10072.2177@compuserve.com
A Study of the Business Support Services Sector, April
1996 (for Department of Trade & Industry)

Rank Xerox Business Services
Bridge House
Oxford Road
Uxbridge, Middx. UB8 1HS
UK
Tel: +44 1895 251133
Fax: +44 1895 254 095

Sanders & Sidney plc
Orion House
5 Upper St. Martin's Lane
London WC2H 9EA
UK
Tel: +44 171 413 0321
Fax: +44 171 497 0380

Terry Smith
Chi-Chi's International (CCI)
Steenweg op Brussel, 541 – Box 1
B-3090 Overijse
Belgium

Outsourcing

Tel: +32 2 657 05 55
Fax: +32 2 657 02 47

John Emerson
Sun Alliance
Stane Court
Albion
Horsham
West Sussex RH12 1FB
UK
Tel: +44 1403 234601
Fax: +44 1403 235750

Texaco Ltd
Corporate Services Department
1 Westferry Circus
Canary Wharf
London E14 4HA
UK
Tel: +44 171 719 3000
Fax: +44 171 719 5130

Typhoon Software
6 East Arrellaga Street
Santa Barbara CA 93101-2502
USA
Tel: +1 805 966 7633
Fax: +1 805 962 6811
E-Mail: typhoon@typhoon.com
WWW: http://www.typhoon.com

Luk Van Wassenhove
INSEAD
Boulevard de Constance
F-77305 Fontainebleau Cedex
France
Tel: +33 1 60 72 40 00
Fax: + 33 1 60 72 42 42
E-mail: Wassenhove@INSEAD.fr

Sean Watson
Typhoon Software
6 East Arrellaga Street
Santa Barbara CA 93101-2502
USA

Outsourcing resource list

Tel: +1 805 966 7633
Fax: +1 805 962 6811
E-Mail: typhoon@typhoon.com
WWW: http://www.typhoon.com

Kevan Wooden
European Controller
Procord
2 The Briars
Waterberry Drive
Waterlooville
Hampshire PO7 7YH
UK
Tel: +44 1705 230 500
Fax: +44 1705 230 501

Xephon Plc
27-35 London Road
Newbury
Berks. RG14 1JK
UK
Tel: +44 1635 33823
Fax: + 44 1635 38345
E-mail: 100325.3711@compuserve.com or
info@xephon.co.uk
WWW: http://www.xephon.co.uk

Appendix B   References

Asbrand, D., 'Outsourcing: managing pieces of the enterprise', *Information Week*, 14 August 1995

Auerbach, J., ' "Outsourcing" is a low-profile way to high-tech profits', *The Boston Globe*, 1996

Baker, R., 'The Backholders', *International Herald Tribune* (Observer), 17 April 1996

Bloomberg Business News, 'GM facing tough contract sessions, job security and outsourcing are key issues in UAW talks', *International Herald Tribune*, 8 July 1996

Business Week, 'Has outsourcing gone too far?', 1 April 1996

Buss, D. D., 'Growing more by doing less', *Nation's Business*, **83**, No. 12, December, 18(5), 1995

Cane, A., 'Tapping into outsourcing', *Financial Times*, 5 July 1996

Carrington, L., 'Outside Chances', *Personnel Today*, 8 February 1994

Case, J., 'The age of the specialist', Inc., **17**, No. 11, August, 15(2), 1995

Chabrow, E. R., *Network Outsourcing*, CMP Publications, 16 October, 1995, Issue 580, p. 41

*'Outsourcing, redefining the corporation of the future', *Fortune*, 12 December, 1994

*'Outsourcing, how industry leaders are reshaping the American corporation', *Fortune*, 16 October, 1995

Outsourcing resource list

Corbett, M. and Lever, S., 'HR concerns in implementing outsourcing agreements,' *Rethinking the HR Function*

Cox C., 'Customers are becoming choosier about services', *Financial Times*, 3 April, 1996

Dawe, T., 'Bids battle for managers on parade', *The Times*, 22 March, 1996

Facilities management, ' A way through the IT maze', June 1996, pp. 20–21

Goldsmith, J., 'When "outsourcing" means "out of a job"?' *Network News*, VNU Publications, 1996

Griggs, R., 'Inside out', *Sales & Marketing Management*, **147**, No. 8, August, 52(6), 1995

Human Resources, 'Inside outsourcing, a special report on the hows and whys for HR Managers', Jan./Feb. 1995 pp. 59–90

James, B., 'Air express services: wings of globalized trade', *International Herald Tribune*, 26 July, 1996

Lowe, K., 'The international market is hotting up', *The Times*, 22 March 1996

Luttwak, E., 'Capitalism's path to intolerance', *World Press Review*, **43**, No. 1, January, 47(2), 1996

Marsh, P., 'A sitting target for two rivals', *The Financial Times*, 15 April 1996

Moran, N., 'From shotgun marriage to love affair', *The Financial Times*, 3 April 1996

Nation's Business, 'Small firms, big clients', **83**, No. 12, December, 22(1), 1995

Nation's Business, 'Virtual companies, real profits', **83**, No. 12, December, 21(1), 1995

Quinn, J.B. and Hilmer, F. G., 'Strategic outsourcing', *The McKinsey Quarterly*, No.1, 1995

Rao, S.S., 'When in doubt, outsource', *Financial World*, **164**, No. 25, December, 77(2), 1995

Reddish, J. J., *How to make 'Outsourcing' Work For You?*, Advent management International Ltd, 1995

... in brief

Outsourcing

Sloane, R., 'Confidentiality, outsourcing and the library', *New York Law Journal* p.5, col.1

Strassmann, P., 'Outsourcing: a game for losers', *Computerworld*, 21 August 1995

Tesler, J., ' Managing logistics in a global market', *Latin American Management*, 1996

Thames, G., 'Outsourcing global telecommunications', *Global Management*, 1994

Tristram, C., 'Stalking the mega outsourcing deal', *Opencomputing*, March 1995

Vrancken, R., 'Outsourcing, insourcing or resourcing? Exploring outsourcing as a process', *Official Journal*, **12**

Williamson, M., 'If the Internet explosion caught you unprepared to field the dazzling Web site with resources on-hand outsourcing may be the way to go', *WebMaster*, Sept./Oct. 1995

Index